PROJECT MAGNET
The Lights In The Sky Are Not Stars

Wilbert Smith, John Musgrave and Grant Cameron
With A Special Introduction By Timothy Green Beckley

PROJECT MAGNET
The Lights In The Sky Are Not Stars
By
Wilbert Smith, John Musgrave and Grant Cameron
With A Special Introduction By Timothy Green Beckley

Published by Global Communications/Conspiracy Journal
Box 753 · New Brunswick, NJ 08903

Staff Members
Timothy G. Beckley, Publisher
Carol Ann Rodriguez, Assistant to the Publisher
Sean Casteel, General Associate Editor
Tim R. Swartz, Graphics and Editorial Consultant
William Kern, Editorial and Art Consultant

Sign Up On The Web For Our Free Weekly Newsletter
and Mail Order Version of Conspiracy Journal
and Bizarre Bazaar
www.ConspiracyJournal.com

Credit Card Order Hot Line: 1-732-602-3407
PayPal: MrUFO8@hotmail.com

Photo credit:
Ottawa New Sciences Club

Wilbert Smith

Conspiracy Journal
PRODUCTIONS

THE BOYS FROM TOPSIDE

THE LIFE OF NEW AGE FUTURIST
WILBERT SMITH

EDITED BY TIMOTHY GREEN BECKLEY & OTTAWA NEW SCIENCES CLUB

Original art by
Carol Ann Rodriguez
from earlier edition.

Original art by
Gene Duplantier
from earlier edition.

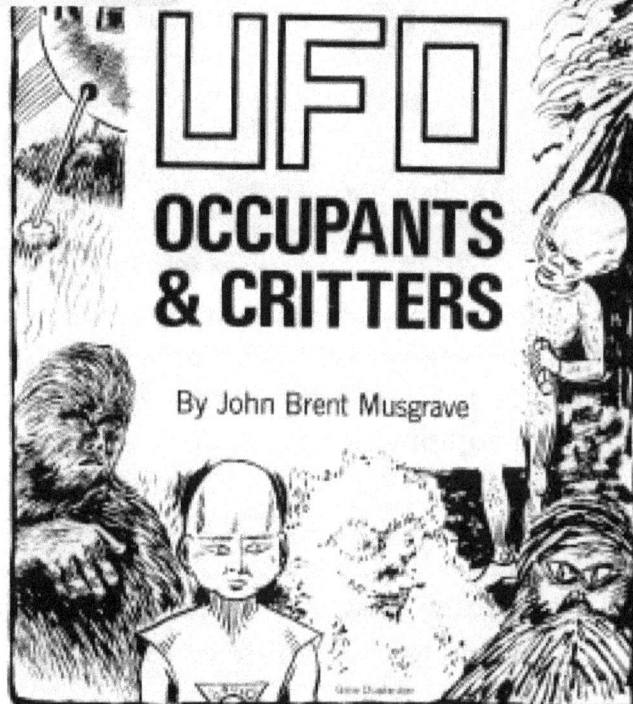

UFO
OCCUPANTS
& CRITTERS

By John Brent Musgrave

v

Machine 'Records Saucer'

OTTAWA — (CP) — Is Canada the first country in the world to record a flying saucer with instruments?

That question is being debated here today after the transport department's flying saucer sighting station reported that it had detected an unexplained object in the atmosphere over Ottawa Sunday.

Wilbert B. Smith, engineer in charge of the broadcast and measurement section of the transport department, said the saucer station's gravimeter was tripped at 3:01 p.m.

The gravimeter is designed to detect and record gamma rays, magnetic fluctuations, radio noises and gravity and mass changes in the atmosphere.

Smith's geo-magnetic studies grew, and in 1952 the investigation was moved to Shirley's Bay, a government facility on the Ottawa River approximately 15km west of Ottawa. UFO detection equipment was installed and by the end of October of 1952 the installation was complete. It became the world's first UFO research facility. The 12 foot by 12 foot building housed instruments such as a gamma-ray counter, a magnetometer, a radio receiver (to detect the presence of radio noise) and a recording gravimeter with a 50 mile radius from the station.

Newspaper article describing the new UFO monitoring station built at Shirley's Bay, Ottawa.

HE HAD WHAT IT TAKES TO BE ADMITTED INTO THE UFO HALL OF FAME
By Timothy Green Beckley

UFOlogy – the study of Uniden-tified Flying Objects, for the uninitiated – does not have a "hall of fame," or even an honor roll as such. And I suspect if it did there would be all sorts of internal disputes about who should be elevated to such a lofty position and who should be left out into the cold.

In the corridors of flying saucer research there is little agreement on any aspect of the topic. It's every man, woman and Ultra-terrestrial to their own cor-ner of the "cosmic ring" in what can easily turn into a cage match like you would expect to see at a WWE "Summer Slam" event.

But, there is one individual that I would lay Vegas odds would not get the cold shoulder treatment. He is Wilbert B. Smith a pioneer in the study of unex-plained aerial phenomena and the primary subject of this book. Almost forgotten these days, Smith was a highly-educated engineer who coaxed the Canadian gov-ernment into establishing Project Magnet, a threadbare project to study and treat reports of UFOs seriously so as to determine who – or what – might be behind this mysterious phenomena that was seemingly taking over the skies of North America after the end of the Second World War.

PROJECT MAGNET

In 1969 Gray Barker's Saucerian Press published a critique of Wilber Smith material which I amassed under the title "The Boys From Topside." I have to say in all candor that it was not one of my early best sellers, though it did foster some decent reviews such as the following remarks from Our Elder Brothers Return, a fringe-sounding think tank: *"The original, well-engineered, 1969 edition (is a) compilation of 11 articles which Canadian engineer, leader of Project Magnet, UFO researcher and contactee Wilbert B. Smith wrote for Topside, the publication of the Ottawa New Sciences Club which he founded. Many of the articles were first reprinted in Flying Saucer Review from the late 1950s onward. The name Topside is derived from Smith's favorite nickname for the space people — 'the boys topside,' a maritime term denoting the personnel on deck. This volume has an introduction by George Hunt Williamson, best known as the author of "Other Tongues, Other Flesh,"a note about the author by the compiler, Timothy Green Beckley, and a foreword by the editors of Topside, titled 'The Space Brothers' Philosophy - and Wilbert B. Smith'. Appended are several related articles by other Topside contributors and/or from other publications.*

A reprint was published in 1996 as 'The Boys From Topside: The Life of New Age Futurist Wilbert Smith' by Inner Light/Global Communications, with a different cover (by Carol Ann Rodriguez)."

Smith was virtually unknown outside of his native Canada and it wasn't until recent years that he became associated with the Roswell UFO incident and is believed to have had conversations with US authorities on the matter, during which they acknowledged they had in their possession wreckage of what is presumed by many to have been a spaceship that came down in New Mexico's dusty heartland. Now, seemingly everyone wants to know all they can about Smith – and we can provide them with what they are looking for in this extreme update of that original manuscript that I edited for a bantam UFO press decades ago.

As part of this essential "modification," I have added relevant material from numerous contributors, as well as from both new and archival sources. Grant Cameron (the only provider of reliable "Disclosure" updates as far as I am concerned) is a vast depository of knowledge on Smith, being a Canuck himself, and has been exceedingly helpful in my compilation. And since Smith is certainly the most important figure in Canadian UFO history, no work on Project Magnet, as far as I am concerned, would be complete without a little known manuscript I personally published in 1979 by John Musgrave which is a chronicle of humanoid and critter encounters North of the American side of the border. I was upset to learn Musgrave went into spirit a number of years ago. His work is one of the best catalogs of UFO encounters of the third kind ever published, and it certainly should be shared with contemporary researchers of UFO lore, as it makes the subject of Project Magnet as complete as it could possibly be, going so far as having been financed by a grant for $6,000 from official sources in Ottawa, the seat of the Canadian authority.

PROJECT MAGNET

Your vibes on this work and others we have published are certainly welcome.

Tim Beckley
mrufo8@hotmail.com
www.ConspiracyJournal.Com
Visit Our YouTube Channel
"Mr UFOs Secret Files"

PROJECT MAGNET

PROJECT MAGNET

In 1950 the Canadian government authorized a short-lived program designed to study UFOs. Here is the program's report by Wilbert B. Smith, Engineer-in-Charge, Project Magnet:

During the past five years there has been accumulating in the files of the United States Air Force, Royal Canadian Air Force, Department of Transport, and various other agencies, an impressive number of reports on sightings of unidentified flying objects, popularly known as "Flying Saucers." These files contain reports by creditable people on things which they have seen in the sky, tracked on radar, or photographed. They are reports made in good faith by normal, honest people, and there is little, if any, reason to doubt their veracity. Many sightings undoubtedly are due to unusual views of common objects or phenomena, and are quite normal, but there are many sightings which cannot be explained so easily.

Project Magnet was authorized in December, 1950, by Commander C. P. Edwards, then Deputy Minister of Transport for Air Services, for the purpose of making as detailed a study of the saucer phenomena as could be made within the framework of existing establishments. The Broadcast and Measures Sections of Telecommunications Division were given the directive to go ahead with this work with whatever assistance could be obtained informally from outside sources such as Defense Research Board and National Research Council.

It is perfectly natural in the human thinking mechanism to try and fit observations into an established pattern. It is only when observations stubbornly refuse to be so fitted that we become disturbed. When this happens we may, and usually do, take one of three courses. First, we may deny completely the validity of the observations; or second, we may pass the whole subject off as something of no consequence; or third, we may accept the discrepancies as real and go to work on them. In the matter of Saucer Sightings, all three of these reactions have been strikingly apparent. The first two approaches are obviously negative and from which a definite conclusion can never be reached. It is the third approach, acceptance of the data and subsequent research that is dealt with in this report.

The basic data with which we have to work consist largely of sightings reported as they are observed throughout Canada in a purely random manner. Many of the reports are from the extensive field organization of the Department of Transport whose job it is to watch the sky and whose observers are trained in precisely this sort of observation. Also, there are in operation a number of instrumental arrangements, such as the ionospheric observatories, from which useful data have been obtained. However, we must not expect too much from these field stations because of the very sporadic nature of the sightings. As the analysis progresses and we know more about what to look for we may be able to obtain and make much better use of field data. Up to the present we have been prevented from using conventional laboratory methods owing to the complete lack of any sort of specimens with which to experiment, and our prospects of obtaining any in the immediate future are not very good. Consequently, a large part of the analysis in these early stages will have to be based on deductive reasoning, at least until we are able to work out a procedure more in line with conventional experimental methods.

The starting point of the investigation is essentially the interview with an observer. A questionnaire form and an instructional guide for the interrogator were worked out by the Project Second Storey Committee, which was a Committee sponsored by the Defense Research Board to collect, catalogue and correlate data on sightings of unidentified flying objects. This questionnaire and guide are included as Appendix I (Editor's Note: This appendix is not included here), and are intended to get the maximum useful information from the observer and present it in a manner which can be used to our advantage. This form has been used so far as possible in connection with the sightings investigated by the Department of Transport.

A weighting factor is assigned to each sighting according to a system intended to minimize the personal equation. This weighting system is described in Appendix II, (Editor's Note: This appendix is not included here). The weighting factor may be considered as the probability that the report contains the truth, the whole truth and nothing but the truth, so far as the observer and interrogator are aware. It has nothing to do with the nature of the object claimed to be seen. It is in a sense analogous to the order of precision with which a measurement may be made, and for the purpose of this analysis this is precisely the manner in which it is used.

Sightings may be grouped according to certain salient features, and the combined weight of all pertinent observations with respect to these features may be determined by applying Peter's formula, which is a standard mathematical technique for determining probable error.

$$r o = \frac{,8453}{n \text{ [sq. root of] } n\text{-}1} \quad (v + v + v + \dots v) \atop \quad\quad\quad\quad\quad\quad 1 \;\; 2 \;\; 3 \quad\;\; n$$

Where "ro" is the probable error of the mean, "n" is the number of observations and "v" is the probable error of each observation, that is, unity minus the weighting factor. This method has the advantage of being simple and easy to use and enables a number of mediocre observations to be combined effectively into the equivalent of one good one.

The next step is to sort out the observations according to some pattern. The particular pattern is not important as the fact that it should take account of all contingencies, however improbable they may appear at first sight. In other words, there must be a compartment somewhere in the scheme of things into which each sighting may be placed, comfortably, and with nothing left over. Furthermore, it must be possible to arrive at each appropriate compartment by a sequence of logical reasoning taking account of all the facts presented. If this can be done, then the probability for the real existence of the contents of any compartment will be the single or combined weighting factor pertinent to that single or group of sightings. The charts shown in Appendix III (Editor's Note: This appendix is not included here) were evolved as a means for sorting out the various sightings and provide the pattern which was used in the analysis of those sightings reported to and analyzed by the Department of Transport.

Most sightings fit readily into one of the classifications shown, which are of two general types; those about which we know something and those about which we know very little. When the sightings can be classified as something we know about, we need not concern ourselves too much with them, but, when they fit into classifications which we don't understand, we are back to our original position of whether to deny the evidence, dismiss it as of no consequence, or to accept it and go to work on it. The process of sorting out observations according to these charts and fitting them into compartments can hardly be considered an end in itself. Rather, it is a convenience to clarify thinking and direct activity along profitable channels. It shows at once which aspects are of significance and which may be bypassed. Merely placing a sighting under a certain heading does not explain it; it only indicates where we may start looking for an explanation.

Appendix IV (Editor's Note: This appendix is not included here) contains summaries of the 1952 sightings as investigated by the Department of Transport. Considerably more data exists in the files of other agencies, and more is being collected as the investigations proceed. While it is not intended to make any reference to an analysis of the records of other agencies, it may be said that the Department of Transport sightings are quite representative of the sightings reported throughout the world. The following is a table of the breakdown of the 25 proper sightings reported during 1952.

PROJECT MAGNET

NATURE OF SIGHTING	NUMBER	WEIGHT
Probably meteor	4	91%
Probably aircraft	1	60%
Probably balloons	1	74%
Probably marker light	1	64%
Bright speck at night, not star or planet	3	75%
Bright speck daylight, not star or planet	1	68%
Luminous ring	1	68%
Shiny cone	1	53%
Circular or elliptical body, shiny day	5	88%
Circular or elliptical body luminous night	5	90%
Unidentified lights of various kinds	2	77%
TOTAL NUMBER OF PROPER SIGHTINGS	25	96%

With reference to the above table, of the four cases identified as probably meteors, their weight works out at 91%, which is the probability that the observers actually did see meteors which appeared as they described them. Considering the circular or elliptical bodies together, their weight works out at 91% for the ten sightings, from which we may conclude that SOMETHING answering this description was actually observed. Similarly we may consider each of the other groups of sightings, taking account of the probability that the observations are reliable.

It is not intended to describe here in detail the intricate and tedious processes by which the sightings are evaluated, beyond the fact that the pattern set forth in the charts in Appendix III (Editor's Note: This appendix is not included here) is followed. The cardinal rule is that a sighting must fit completely under one or more of the chart headings, with nothing left over and without postulating any additions, deletions, or changes in the facts reported. Should there be no suitable heading, then obviously the charts must be expanded to provide one; in fact, this was the evolution of these charts. Where a sighting may be fitted under more than one heading, an arbitrary division of the probability of finding it under each applicable heading is assigned. The sum of such probability figures must of course be unity, and the probability for the real existence under any particular heading is the product of this probability figure and the reliability or weighting factor for the sighting concerned.

It is apparent that the judgment of the people doing the evaluating is bound to enter the picture and may produce substantial numerical differences with reference to sightings listed under certain headings. However, since many headings are automatically eliminated by the nature of the facts available, the discrepancies are confined to the probability figures for the distribution under the remaining headings which are considered eligible, and we end up with definite classifications for the sightings with SOME probability figure for the reality of each group. This has the effect of forcing those who are doing the evaluating to face the reported facts squarely, pay meticulous attention to them, and place each sighting honestly under the only heading where it will fit.

In working through the analysis of the proper sightings listed, we find the majority of them appear to be of some material body. Of these, seven are classed as probably normal objects, and eleven are classed as strange objects. Of the remainder, four have a substantial probability of being material, strange, objects, with three having a substantial probability of being immaterial, electrical, phenomena. Of the eleven strange objects, the probability definitely favors the alien vehicle class, with the secret missile included with a much lower probability.

The next step is to follow this line of reasoning as far as possible so as to deduce what we can from the observed data. Vehicles or missiles can be of only two general kinds, terrestrial and extraterrestrial, and in either case the analysis enquires into the source and technology. If the vehicles originate outside the Iron Curtain, we may assume that the matter is in good hands, but, if they originate inside the Iron Curtain, it could be a matter of grave concern to us.

In the matter of technology, the points of interest are: – the energy source; means of support, propulsion and manipulation; structure; and biology. So far as energy is concerned, we know about mechanical energy and chemical energy, and a little about energy of fission, and we can appreciate the possibility of direct conversion of mass to energy. Beyond this we have no knowledge, and unless we are prepared to postulate a completely unknown source of energy of which we do not know even the rudiments, we must conclude that the vehicles use one of the four listed sources. Unless something we do not understand can be done with gravitation, mechanical energy has little use beyond driving model aircraft. We use chemical energy to quite an extent, but we realize its limitations, so if the energy demands of the vehicles exceed what we consider to be the reasonable capabilities of chemical fuels, we are forced to the conclusion that such vehicles must get their energy from either fission or mass conversion.

With reference to the means for support, propulsion and manipulation, unless we are prepared to postulate something quite beyond our knowledge, there are only two groups of possibilities, namely the known means and the speculative means. Of the known means there is only physical support through the use of buoyancy or airfoils, the reaction of rockets and jets, and centrifugal force, which is what holds the moon in position. Of the speculative means we know only of the possibility of gravity waves, field interaction and radiation pressure. If the observed behavior of the vehicles is such as to be beyond the limitations which we know apply to the known means of support, then we are forced to the conclusion that one of the speculative means must have been developed to do the job.

From a study of the sighting reports (Appendix IV) (Editor's Note: This appendix is not included here), it can be deduced that the vehicles have the following significant characteristics. They are a hundred feet or more in diameter; they can travel at speeds of several thousand miles per hour; they can reach altitudes well above those which would support conventional aircraft or balloons; and ample power and force seem to be available for all required maneuvers. Taking these factors into account, it is difficult to reconcile this performance with the capabilities of our technology, and unless the technology of some terrestrial nation is much more advanced than is generally known, we are forced to the conclusion that the vehicles are probably extraterrestrial, in spite of our prejudices to the contrary.

It has been suggested that the sightings might be due to some sort of optical phenomenon which gives the appearances of the objects being reported, and this aspect was thoroughly investigated. Charts are shown in Appendix III (Editor's Note: This appendix is not included here) showing the various optical considerations. Enticing as this theory is, there are some serious objections to its actual application, in the form of some rather definite and quite immutable optical laws. These are geometrical laws dealing with optics generally and which we have never yet found cause to doubt, plus the wide discrepancies in the order of magnitude of the light values which must be involved in any sightings so far studied. Furthermore, introducing an optical system might explain an image in terms of an object, but the object still requires explaining. A particular effort was made to find an optical explanation for the sightings listed in this report, but in no case could one be worked out. It was not possible to find so much as a partial optical explanation for even one sighting. Consequently, it was felt that optical theories generally should not be taken too seriously until such time as at least one sighting can be satisfactorily explained in such a manner.

PROJECT MAGNET

It appears then, that we are faced with a substantial possibility of the real existence of extraterrestrial vehicles, regardless of whether or not they fit into our scheme of things. Such vehicles of necessity must use a technology considerably in advance of what we have. It is therefore submitted that the next step in this investigation should be a substantial effort towards the acquisition of a much as possible of this technology, which would no doubt be of great value to us.

(original signed)

W. B. Smith,

Engineer-in-Charge

Project Magnet

PROJECT MAGNET

The following article is posted here courtesy of The Disclosure Project:

(Editor's Note: The document we worked from was a graphical capture of a somewhat poor original. There are a number of words in the following text that we simply couldn't make out clearly enough. In those cases we will simply insert "(unreadable"). I think the remaining text, while incomplete, is still a very significant document for any student of ufology.

This memorandum was written by Wilbert Smith on November 21, 1950,

To the Controller of Telecommunications:

For the past several years we have been engaged in the study of various aspects of radio wave propagation. The vagaries of this phenomenon have led us into the fields of aurora, oceanic radiation, atmospheric radioactivity and geo-magnetism. In the case of geo-magnetics, our investigations have contributed little to our knowledge of radio wave propagation as yet, but nevertheless have indicated several avenues of investigation which may well be explored with profit. For example, we are on the track of a means whereby the potential energy of the earth's magnetic field ray may be abstracted and used.

On the basis of theoretical considerations, a small and very crude experimental unit was constructed approximately a year ago and tested in our standards laboratory. The tests were essentially successful in that sufficient energy was abstracted from the earth's field to operate a voltmeter, approximately 50 millewatts. Although this unit was far from being self-sustaining, it nevertheless demonstrated the soundness of the basic principles in a qualitative manner and provided useful data for the design of a better unit.

The design has now been completed for a unit which should be self-sustaining and in addition provide a small surplus of power. Such a unit, in addition to functioning as a "pilot power plant," should be large enough to permit the study of the various reaction forces which are expected to develop.

We believe that we are on the track of something which may well prove to be the introduction of new technology. The existence of a different technology is borne out by the investigations which are being carried on at the present time in relation to flying saucers.

While in Washington attending the NARS Conference, two books (3 words unreadable) "Flying Saucers Are Real" by Donald Keyhoe. Both books dealt mostly with sightings of unidentified objects and both books claim that flying objects were of extraterrestrial origin and might well be spaceships from another planet. (Unreadable) claimed that the preliminary studies of one saucer that fell into the hands of the United States Government indicated that they operated on some hitherto unknown magnetic principles. It appeared to me that our own work in geo-magnetics might well be the linkage between our technology and the technology by which the saucers are designed and operated. If it is assumed that our geo-magnetic investigations are in the right direction, the theory of operation of the saucers becomes quite straightforward, with all observed features explained qualitatively and quantitatively.

I made discreet enquiries through the Canadian Embassy staff in Washington who were able to obtain for me the following information:

1.   The matter is the most highly classified subject in the United States Government, rating even higher than the A-bomb.

2.   Flying saucers exist.

3.   Their modus operandi is unknown but concentrated effort is being made by a small group headed by Doctor (unreadable) Bush.

4.   The entire matter is considered by the United States authorities to be of tremendous significance.

I was further informed that the United States authorities are investigating along quite a number of lines which might possibly be related to the (unreadable) such as mental phenomena and I gather that they are not doing too well since they indicated that if Canada is doing anything at all in geo-magnetics they would welcome a discussion with suitably accredited Canadians.

While I am not yet in a position to say that we have solved even the first problems in geo-magnetic energy release, I feel that the correlation between our basic theory and the available information on saucers checks too closely to be mere coincidence. It is my honest opinion that we are on the right track and are fairly close to at least some of the answers.

Mr. (unreadable), Defence Research Board liaison officer at the Canadian Embassy in Washington, was extremely anxious for me to get in touch with Doctor (unreadable), Chairman of the Defence Research Board, to discuss with him future investigations along the lines of geo-magnetic energy release. I do not feel that we have as yet sufficient data to place before Defence Research Board which would enable a program to be initiated within that organization, but I do feel that further work of our own organization with, of course, full cooperation and exchange of information with other interested bodies.

PROJECT MAGNET

I discussed this matter fully with Doctor (unreadable), Chairman of Defence Research Board, on November 20th and placed before him as much information as I have been able to gather to date. Doctor (unreadable) agreed that work on geo-magnetic energy should go forward as rapidly as possible and offered full cooperation of his Board in providing laboratory facilities, acquisition of necessary items of equipment, and specialized personnel for incidental work in the project. I indicated to Doctor (unreadable) that we would prefer to keep the project with the Department of Transport for the time being until we have obtained sufficient information to permit a complete assessment of the value of our work.

It is therefore recommended that a PROJECT be set up within the framework of this Section to study this problem and that the work be carried on a part-time basis until such time as sufficient tangible results can be seen to warrant more definitive action. Cost of the program in its initial stages are expected to be less than a few hundred dollars and can be carried by our Radio Standards Lab appropriation.

Attached hereto is a draft of terms of reference for such a project, which, if authorized, will enable us to proceed with this research work within our own organization.

(W. B. Smith)
Senior Radio Engineer

PROJECT MAGNET

CANADIAN PROGRAM DIRECTOR DISCUSSES
COMMUNICATION WITH ALIENS

"In 1950 I was attending a rather slow-moving broadcasting conference in Washington D.C. and, having some free time on my hands, I circulated around asking a few questions about flying saucers, which stirred up a hornet's nest. I found that the U. S. government had a highly classified project set up to study them, so I reasoned that with so much smoke maybe I should look for the fire." Wilbert Smith, Official Director of the Canadian Government's UFO Investigation - 1950-1954

In a just-recovered 1961 interview with television station CJOH, the former head of the official Canadian Government UFO investigation, Wilbert Smith, was asked a number of questions about what he had learned during his days of investigating flying saucers for the government. Among the many questions was one about whether or not communication had taken place "between space people and people of this planet," and if communication had occurred – how was it done?

The question of communication addressed to Smith was important, not only because he headed up the official government investigation into UFOs from 1950 – 1954, but because Smith was one of the foremost communications experts of the day.

Smith worked as the chief radio engineer for the Canadian government, going on in 1956 to head up the country's radio regulations department. More importantly, he was in charge of monitoring 50,000 radio frequencies in Canada, and ran the Top Secret "Radio Ottawa" where spies would radio in to intelligence services.

Smith's reply to the interviewer regarding the subject of talking to aliens was positive.

"Some of the communications have been on a face-to-face basis but I have not been so honored myself. Some of the communications have been by ordinary radio, and I have received a few messages by this means. But by far the majority of the communications are by what we call Tensor Beam transmission, which uses a type of radio with which we are only vaguely familiar, and which I couldn't possibly attempt to describe now. However, the mental images of the person wishing to transmit are picked up, electrically amplified, and modulated into a tensor beam, which is directed to the person to whom the transmission is addressed, and within whose brain the mental images are recreated. The transmissions are therefore very precise, and independent of language. I have had some experience with these transmissions myself and can say that they are like nothing within the conventional experiences of earth people."

In the rest of the interview Wilbert Smith discusses what the aliens look like, the effect of the extraterrestrial idea on religion, secrecy, and a number of other topics. It should be noted in the interview that Wilbert Smith never used the word UFO. This is because from the very beginning Smith was aware that the phenomena was extraterrestrial, and that UFO was a word developed by the U.S.A.F. in 1952 to muddy the waters for investigators. According to Smith's son, Jim Smith, shortly before his death in 1962 Wilbert called his son in, and told him that he had in fact seen the alien bodies from a crash, and had been shown a crashed flying saucer outside of Washington D.C., while conducting the official Canadian investigation. The 1961 interview continues.

Q: Do you believe that flying saucers are real?

A: Yes. I am convinced that they are just as real and tangible as most things we deal with in our everyday lives.

Q: Why do you think they are real?

A: Because thousands of people have seen them, many under circumstances which virtually preclude misinterpretation, and many of these sightings have been coordinated with radar fixes. Photographs have been taken and physical evidence has been accumulated.

Q: Have you ever seen a flying saucer yourself?

A: I have seen several objects which I concluded were flying saucers simply because they couldn't be anything else.

Q: Would you please describe such a sighting?

A; Last year, I think it was August 16, (Echo 1 was launched August 12, 1960) right after the launching of Echo I, my wife and I, and a couple of friends, were outside sky-gazing to see the passage of Echo 1 which was due about ten minutes to nine. At about a quarter to nine a bright object came from the south at an apparent speed about twice the expected speed of Echo, and traveled almost due north. As it approached, and when viewed through binoculars, it appeared to be a steady brilliant white light with a flashing electric blue light superimposed on it. At first the rate of flashing was not apparent as it was above the flicker frequency, but as it approached the frequency of the flicker slowed down until it was about one per second as it passed overhead. As it proceeded northward it suddenly made a sharp right hand turn and headed due west and disappeared into the western sky, with the blue light still flashing. There was no noise and the apparent speed was about the same as a jet flying at 10,000 feet. About five or so minutes later Echo 1 sailed majestically into view from the southwest at much less than half the apparent speed of the previous object.

Q: Where you able to see any shape of the object?

A: No. Just a bright white light, with the intense blue light with it.

Q: You said earlier that there was physical evidence, and that pictures existed supporting the reality of flying saucers. Would you please explain?

A: There have been over a hundred books and very many magazines published in the last ten or twelve years, the majority of which are predominately accounts of sightings, pictures, and descriptions of the physical evidence, which has accumulated. In the limited time available I could not possibly cover more than one or two such cases. However, here are a couple of interesting ones. (Two book quotes)

Q: Have you, yourself, actually handled any material believed to be from a flying saucer?

A: If by that you mean material substance showing evidence of fabrication through intelligent effort and not originating on this planet, I have. But I cannot say from my own knowledge that it was ever part of a flying saucer. Unfortunately, most of my contacts in this direction were through classified channels, which for some particular reason, which I could never fathom, insisted on "Classifying" these matters, and I am not at liberty to discuss them further.

Q: What about pictures?

A: I am naturally very skeptical about pictures since they are so very easy to fake. So unless I have taken the picture myself and participated in its developing, I would not like to offer any of them as authentic. I have taken a few myself, but I'm afraid that they are not very impressive. There are, however, many pictures available, which, whether they are fakes or not, do check quite well with the many visual descriptions. Here are a few. (Shows a few photographs)

Q: How long have you been studying flying saucers?

A: I suppose I have always known that there were other intelligent beings in the universe other than ourselves, and that sooner or later they would visit us. In 1947, when the first widespread publicity on flying saucers came about, I thought this was something worth thinking about and maybe investigating. However, I didn't get around to active participation until 1950, when I was attending a rather slow-moving broadcasting conference in Washington D.C. and having some free time on my hands, I circulated around asking a few questions about flying saucers, which stirred up a hornet's nest. I found that the U.S. government had a highly classified project set up to study them, so I reasoned that with so much smoke maybe I should look for the fire. So I set about gathering as much sighting data as I could get ahold of and analyzing it, from which I concluded that there was a 91% probability that the saucers were real, and a 60% probability that they were alien craft of some kind.

Q: What is the "official" view of flying saucers?

A: I don't even know if there is one, in Canada. In the United States there have been so many contradictory statements made that I doubt if anyone could sort them out. However, I don't think it really matters much anyway because the saucers are here and our opinions regarding them are not going to change matters. It has been my experience that no one who takes even a little time to study the evidence available publicly remains skeptic very long. This is quite apart from those who have had access and studied the larger files of evidence collected by private and semiofficial organizations.

Q: How widespread is the interest in flying saucers?

A: I really don't know, but I think that most people are prepared to take them in their stride, along with atomic energy and earth-circling satellites. I have encountered very few really dyed in the wool skeptics. Judging from the large number of saucer clubs, one or two in each city, and the number of publications available, I would say that the interest was considerable.

Q: Since you say that you have been active in the study of flying saucers for over ten years, what have you found out about them?

A: That is a tall order and would take a good many hours. Most of it is available in reliable bookstores anyway, so I only propose to cover the highlights here. There is much evidence that people who build and fly flying saucers are people very much like us. They have been seen on many occasions and there are many claims of personal contact having been established with them. Communications with these people tell us that they are our distant relatives; that we are descendants of their colonists on this planet, and that they still regard us as brothers even though we don't often act like it. There is much evidence that the technology of these people is quite a bit ahead of ours, and that through study of the behavior of the saucers and from the alleged communications we have been able to piece together some of this technology, and it is amazing to say the least. We are informed that these people are really civilized, in that they regard all men as brothers; that they do not have wars, and live under conditions of personal freedom of which we cannot conceive.

Q: Have you any indication of why the saucers are here at this time?

A: There is much evidence in history, legend and the Bible, that flying saucers have visited this planet on many occasions in the past and that the present visitation is nothing new; it is simply a bit more intense than in the past and we have better news dissemination means now. I think that these people from elsewhere are concerned with our playing with atomic energy, and about our plans for space travel and interplanetary exploration and conquest. I am sure that they do not hold us in very high esteem, and are worried about what we might do if we ever got loose in space armed to the teeth with nuclear weapons.

Q: Have you any ideas about how flying saucers operate?

A: As I said before, the technology of these people from elsewhere is quite a bit ahead of ours, and they have an understanding of the realities of this universe that we are just approaching. We have started at the effects and speculated towards the causes, whereas they started at the cause and worked towards the effects, with the result that they are not nearly as self-limited in science as we are.

Our observations indicate that the saucers can hover indefinitely in one place, or they can dart off with very high accelerations. Also, they can change direction quickly; all this with utter disregard of the laws of inertia, as we understand them. From this we conclude that they must understand these laws better than we do and have found ways of getting around the situation. Our own work along these lines, aided by tips from outside, indicates that the trick is through gravity control wherein the earth's gravity field is bent to accommodate the action required.

Q: That sounds quite technical, but could you explain it further?

A: I'm afraid not, and I am sure that you will appreciate the reasons, which should be fairly obvious.

Q: I know this may be a hot question, but how do you think flying saucers affect religion?

A: As far as I can determine, these people from elsewhere are a great deal more religious than we are. They believe in a Supreme Creator, the brotherhood and divinity of Man, and a plan for the evolution of all. To these people, their religion is a matter of daily reality, not just Sunday profession, and they certainly seem to practice what we preach. I can find no contradictions with any of the religions of this planet.

Q: Do you have any idea where these people come from?

A: I am informed through the many alleged contacts that these people come from everywhere; that there is no place in the universe where man can live that he does not live.

Q: How about traveling about in the universe? Doesn't it take a terribly long time?

A: I am afraid our ideas about certain things are due for a severe revision in the not too distant future. I am informed that time is not at all what we think it is, but is in fact variable. Also, that the velocity of light is not at all a limiting velocity. It merely appears so to us because we can't see any faster. I understand that these people from elsewhere can and do travel about a great deal and I'm sure they don't take years and years to do it.

Q: You seem to have a great deal of inside information about these things; what are you doing about it? Are you bringing it to the attention of the scientists?

A: I have made no secret of the information with which I am entrusted, and will gladly pass it on to anyone who is sincerely interested and wants to learn. But I feel that I have no obligation whatsoever to force this knowledge on anyone or to interfere in his or her chosen pattern of thinking. I know these things to be true, and all the opinions to the contrary aren't going to change things. When the time is right they will be accepted. In the meantime, I am NOT a missionary. I am concentrating my efforts on increasing my own understanding and the understanding of those who work with me in this area.

** ***

During the 1950s, the world was gripped with paranoia dealing with the threat of nuclear war, and a new phenomenon that was sweeping the world...UFOs. With reports of Unidentified Flying Objects growing each day, both the general public and government agencies from around the world quickly reacted. Canada was not without its own concerns over these new "alien spacecraft" roaming the skies, and set up a special investigation unit in Ottawa under the name "PROJECT MAGNET."

Project Magnet was an unidentified flying object (UFO) study program established by the Canadian Department of Transport (DOT) on December 2, 1950, under the direction of Wilbert B. Smith, senior radio engineer for the DOT's Broadcast and Measurements Section. Smith, the Defence Research Board and the National Research Council (NRC) were trying to determine that, if UFOs did really exist, whether they might hold the key to a new source of power using the earth's magnetic field as a source of propulsion for their vehicles. The top secret project in Ottawa was also working with their American counterparts in the CIA to determine if this new UFO "power source" could be studied and harnessed.

The man who headed Project Magnet at Shirley's Bay, Ottawa, was Wilbert Smith.

Smith's geo-magnetic studies grew, and in 1952 the investigation was moved to Shirley's Bay, a government facility on the Ottawa River approximately 15km west of Ottawa. UFO detection equipment was installed and by the end of October of 1952 the installation was complete. It became the world's first UFO research facility. The 12 foot by 12 foot building housed instruments such as a gamma-ray counter, a magnetometer, a radio receiver (to detect the presence of radio noise) and a recording gravimeter within a 50 mile radius from the station.

Newspaper article describing the new UFO monitoring station built at Shirley's Bay, Ottawa.

UFO Monitoring equipment installed at Shirley's Bay in 1952. It was the world's first UFO detection site.

Smith and his UFO research team at Shirley's Bay conducted a number of experiments trying to attract UFOs to the area using their newly installed equipment. After months of potential UFO activity being recorded in the area, the facility soon had their most unusual occurrence. At 3:01 P.M. on August 8, 1954 the instrumentation at the Shirley's Bay installation registered an unusual disturbance. In Smith's words "the gravimeter went wild," as a much greater deflection was registered than could be explained by conventional interference such as a passing aircraft. Smith and his colleagues rushed outside their research building at Shirley's Bay to view the craft that was creating such an enormous reading on their equipment. Once outside the building, they were disappointed to find a heavily overcast sky with limited visibility. Whatever kind of craft that was up there was well-hidden under the cover of clouds. The only evidence the researchers had of this large UFO was the deflection registered on the chart recorder paper.

Newspaper article describing the event at Shirley's Bay.

Two days later Smith and the Shirley's Bay research facility were abruptly shut down upon orders from the Department Of Transport. Many speculate the findings and strange occurrence at Shirley's Bay prompted the project to go "underground," with all findings entering the "TOP SECRET" status of operation elsewhere. Smith was allowed to remain if he chose to, but all government funding to conduct his UFO research was halted. Without government subsidies. Smith continued his research, funded by "other sources." Smith carried on working at Shirley's Bay, developing what he claimed was a breakthrough antigravity device. In a 1959 presentation Smith stated "We have conducted experiments that show that it is possible to create artificial gravity (not centrifugal force) and to alter the gravitational field of the Earth. This we have done. It is fact. The next step is to learn the rules and do the engineering necessary to convert the principle into workable hardware."

As Smith was about to finish work on this antigravity device, he was stricken with cancer and died at the age of 52 on December 27, 1962. His work on UFOs and antigravity devices came to halt and the research facility at Shirley's Bay was closed. The Project Magnet building he worked in apparently still existed until 2011 at the Shirley's Bay Department of National Defence complex, now known as "Defence Research and Development Canada," off Carling Avenue. It was simply marked as Building 67. His research building off Carling Avenue was torn down in 2011 and nothing remains but an empty lot.

PROJECT MAGNET

WILBERT SMITH, A CRASHED SAUCER,
AND THE ULTIMATE ALIEN ENCOUNTER©

By Grant Cameron

As more and more is made public about the flying saucer research of Canadian Project Magnet Director Wilbert Smith, it becomes more and more apparent that Smith enjoyed a high "need-to-know" on the subject, and at least temporarily held a close relationship with those doing the highest-level research in the United States. Agencies included the CIA, U. S. Navy, FBI, NASA, and the U. S. Research and Development Board.

Wilbert Smith wrote about some of this cooperation in his November 21, 1950, Top Secret UFO memo to the Department of Transport. "They indicated," Smith wrote, "that if Canada is doing anything at all in geo-magnetics, they would welcome a discussion with suitably accredited Canadians."

Vannevar Bush, who Wilbert Smith had described in the Top Secret UFO memo as the head of a small group in the United States making a "concentrated effort" to discover the modus operandi of the flying saucers, also discussed Canadian-U. S. cooperation.

"We must depend heavily on the Canadians for investigation of communication, navigation, projectile control methods and ionospheric measurements in the all-important auroral belt. Interchange of technical information should be uninhibited to enable us to gain necessary Canadian information so that studies of the earth's magnetic field may be completed." [1],[2]

As a strange footnote to the possible exchange of flying saucer secrets from the United States to the Canadians, all disclosure of technical information to foreign nationals was contained in policy document "State-Defense MIC (Military Information Control Committee) 206/29." The committee determined the "various potential countries-recipient and delineated the limits of classification" for each "whether made orally or by means of transfer of reports or other documents."

The Committee had a member from each of the three military services, and there was a fourth member of the committee from the Research and Development Board. Interestingly, the R&DB member for the period 1950-1951 when Smith first interviewed Dr. Robert Sarbacher, wrote his Top Secret UFO memo, and was sending UFO papers to Vannevar Bush, was none other Dr. Eric A. Walker. (At the time Executive Director at the R&DB)

Dr. Walker would go on to give a number of UFO interviews, which became the basis of the book "UFOs, MJ-12, and the Government." If Smith had requested access to the craft and bodies, later interviews with Dr. Walker indicate Walker would have known where to send him.

THE CRASHED SAUCER

The Smith crashed flying saucer story actually goes back to the early 1980s. Alberta researcher John Musgrave told this researcher that Buck Buchanan, a close private associate of Smith in his post-Project Magnet flying saucer research (1954-1961), lived near him and was telling him some incredible stories about his days working with Smith.

In a later letter to this author, Musgrave mentioned the story that Smith claimed he had been given a peek at a flying saucer at a Washington D.C. Air Force Base in the early 1950s. Although Musgrave didn't reveal the source, it seemed certain that this was one of the amazing stories he had been told by Buchanan.

Musgrave stated his belief that he thought Smith might have been caught up in some sort of disinformation, and only thought he had seen a real craft. Musgrave made no reference to alien bodies being involved in the Washington saucer story.

In April, 2002, I interviewed Wilbert Smith's oldest son James and asked him about the crashed flying story told by Buchanan. James Smith confirmed the story, stating that his father had told him the story near the end of his life. What he had been told agreed with Buchanan's Washington Air Force Base version.

THE BODIES

A second item that adds credence to the idea that Smith had been taken into the ultimate inner circle of those who had actually controlled the extraterrestrial proof was a story that Wilbert Smith had actually seen the extraterrestrial bodies from one of the crashes.

PROJECT MAGNET

This genesis of this body story goes back to the Hotel Algonquin in 1972. Psychiatrist and paranormal researcher Dr. Berthold Schwarz was meeting with Harold Sherman, a renowned paragnost, psychic researcher and author of more than 90 books. Sherman was also prominent for his experiments in telepathy conducted between himself in New York City and Sir Hubert Wilkins, who was at the time in the Canadian arctic.

During the conversation with Dr. Schwarz, Sherman began talking about his friendship with Mr. Silas Newton. Newton was the geophysicist and oil businessman who gave the original lecture about the 1948 Aztec, New Mexico crash at the University of Denver on March 8, 1950.

It was also Silas Newton who had approached prominent Hollywood writer Frank Scully with the story of the Aztec crash, which Scully wrote up in a bestselling book called "Behind the Flying Saucers." The book created a stir of controversy and was generally written off by the majority of researchers as a hoax.

Part of the book's problems was that, despite many attempts from researchers, reporters, and people offering movie deals, neither Newton nor Scully would reveal the eight different sources that had provided the details of the Aztec crash.

Harold Sherman had met Newton through Frank Scully, who had been a longtime friend. He went on to know Newton for 30 years and gained great respect for him. He called him "an altogether extraordinary person who probably was misunderstood in many fields, but he had an awful lot to him."[3]

According to Schwarz, it was during the 1972 discussion that Sherman had told him Wilbert Smith had provided access to the Aztec crash bodies for Silas Newton. In his 1983 book "UFO Dynamics," Schwarz wrote "through the intervention of Wilbert Smith, electronics expert and organizer of Project Magnet, Newton later actually saw the humanoids himself."[4]

The significant part of this disclosure is that Newton, although accosted by many researchers as an untrustworthy con man, ended up describing an event that now fits with what we know about Smith.

As well as telling a story that other more reliable people were telling, the story also rings true because if Newton made up the story about seeing the bodies it makes no sense that he would claim to have been given this ultimate Top Secret access through a foreign national. He would surely have claimed access through some high level U. S. official, or through his mysterious group of eight scientists known as "Dr. Gee."

Another fact not known in 1972 when Schwarz and Sherman spoke is the fact that Smith was very interested in the Aztec crash. In 1983, a transcript of a September 1950 interview between Wilbert Smith and a U. S. military scientist by the name of Dr. Robert Sarbacher was released.

In this interview Dr. Robert Sarbacher had told Smith "the facts in the book

(Frank Scully's book on crashed flying saucers) are substantially correct."[5] Smith would therefore have been operating under the assumption that the Aztec crash did take place despite the numerous debunking articles that were being written about the Scully book in the early fifties. There is little doubt that Smith would have followed on Aztec with other high-ranking U. S. officials.

There was no correspondence between Smith and Scully or Newton found in Scully's files at the University of Wyoming, or in the Wilbert Smith files found at the University of Ottawa. Any contact with Newton by Smith would have been by phone or through channels.

The evidence that Smith had seen the bodies continued to surface in a 1997 message published on the Usenet from a former President of the Montreal Flying Saucer Club. This group was very active during the sixties, and it had contacts with the Ottawa Flying Saucer Club just down the road. The two groups had also done work together on two large objects that had been recovered from the shore of the St. Lawrence River in 1961.

The story told by the former president, who identified himself only as The Observer, is that four members of the Montreal group had been visiting Ottawa in early 1964, and that they had stayed overnight at Mrs. Smith's home.

It was during supper during the evening that Mrs. Smith told tales about her former husband. One of the stories included the fact that Wilbert Smith had personally viewed dead alien bodies. In an email to this author The Observer wrote,

"We were told about the bodies that Wilbert Smith had seen when he was personally invited by the US military. We were simply told that he saw the bodies and from the impression that I received it was for only a short time - minutes not hours."[6]

This Montreal Flying Saucer Club member further described the bodies according to what he recalled Mrs. Smith had stated.

"Mr. Smith described (to his wife) the dead occupants as having been approximately 4.5 to 5 feet in height, grayish blue tint to the skin, large eyes, small slit for a mouth and four long fingers with no thumbs."[7]

This large eyes and four finger description is the only time a "grey type" description of the alien was ever associated with Wilbert Smith. The Observer, in relating what Mrs. Smith had told the four Montreal members, might have added more than what they were actually told. For example, in a separate article written by The Observer concerning the disclosures made by Wilbert's wife, the claim was made that the Smith description was associated with Roswell. The article also stated Smith had been invited to the crash site. Smith did not get involved in flying saucers till 1950, so there is no way he was at the Roswell crash site in July 1947. [8]

The large-eyed grey idea was not only unknown to Wilbert Smith, it was also unknown in the UFO world prior to the 1961 abduction of Betty and Barney

Hill. There were tall 7' 8' or 10' beings, little men, small hairy dwarf like beings, dwarflike beings with large heads, entities shaped like potato bags, robot-like creatures, entities without heads, and many, many "humanlike figures."

The days when Wilbert Smith was researching were dominated by contactees, and Wilbert Smith was one himself. In a letter to a Mr. Milne in 1957, for example, Smith stated, "It is my opinion that the people from outside are so much like us that they could mingle with us and we would be none the wiser."

Once Smith died and the Hill abduction gained widespread publicity, all the alien encounters from 1947-1961 were basically removed from UFO histories as if they had never occurred.

Most present day researchers, for example, would probably agree with J. Allen Hynek (Scientific Consultant to the United States Air Force Project Blue Book) who described "most contactees as 'pseudo-religious fanatics of low credibility value,'" [9] or with abduction researcher David Jacobs, who stated "basically contactee followers were gullible people who, through lack of adequate factual information about the UFO phenomena, formulated a belief system that easily incorporated the contactees' claims as fact." [10]

The usual telling of the Smith body story is the one related in 1998, when researcher and author Palmiro Campagna wrote the following in the Postscript section of his 1998 soft cover edition of "The UFO Files." He wrote:

"According to James Smith, on one of his many trips to the U.S. Wilbert Smith told his son that he was shown recovered bodies from a recovered craft. Wilbert Smith described the bodies as small and humanoid in appearance."

In July 2000 I interviewed James Smith by phone and revisited the issue of the alien bodies that Smith had seen. James stated that he had been told about the bodies as his father was near death. James did not recall that the body description involved greys – simply small people.

In March 2002 James Smith was a guest on the "Strange Days . . . Indeed" radio show where he described the UFO hardware his father had received from the United States to analyze, and he again was asked about the alien body story.

James Smith described the aliens as "small humanoid" and "like descriptions of the time." These descriptions were in agreement with descriptions made by many other people having alien encounters in the fifties. They would also agree with Smith's notion that the aliens were not much different than we were and might even be distant relatives.

TIMING

If it occurred, it seems most probable that the Smith viewing of the crashed saucers and bodies occurred in the early fifties. The reasons for that would include:

PROJECT MAGNET

*** Correspondence from the Canadian Embassy in Washington during 1951 indicates that during that period Smith was dealing, at least indirectly, with Vannevar Bush at the Research and Development Board in Washington, D.C. Bush, being the head of the U.S. flying saucer effort, would have been able to give Smith access to craft and bodies.

*** Most importantly, Smith directed the classified Project Magnet from December 1950 to August 1954. With his clearance he would have been in a position to be shown the craft and body. Once the classified program was closed down in August 1954, Smith's clearance and "need-to-know" on flying saucers probably went with it.

*** Prior to the CIA Robertson panel in January 1953, the subject of flying saucers was more openly discussed. It is then more probable Smith was shown the craft and body before the CIA began the debunking campaign.

*** The report from Sherman that Silas Newton was given access to the bodies through Wilbert Smith's help also indicates an early fifties date.

*** The Musgrave story concerning the Washington crashed saucer viewing mentioned the early fifties.

*** The tone of Smith's writings near the end of his life in 1962 was not upbeat. Smith had not received a message from AFFA for almost two years. He had taken his antigravity experiment apart, telling his wife that the world was not ready for it. His writing began to reflect his strong belief that the important part of the UFO mystery was in the philosophy of the aliens rather than in their technological hardware. In the early fifties, Smith's writing had showed a keen interest in discovering the propulsion of the strange new objects.

[1] Memorandum: "Vannevar Bush to Colonel Wood" Research and Development Board Files, National Archives, Box 534, Folder 3. Most of the Canadian contact was made through the liaison of the Research Defense Board of Canada, which was "charged with the establishment of all policies in the field of military research and development as well as exercising the executive functions of administering all the research and development installations in the Military Establishment."

[2] Dr. Omond Solandt, then the head of the Canadian Defense Research Board, has on many occasions denied that this Smith–Bush relationship occurred. In a June 8, 1991, interview with Dr. Henry Victorian, Solandt said, "Not that they (U.S.) were doing any work on it. They were watching it very closely as far as I knew. . . I got my information from Van Bush. At that time I used to see him a couple times during the year, and that was a subject that we sometimes discussed, but we never did any joint work on it."

Solandt was questioned many times about whether or not Smith had worked with the Americans. In early interviews, Solandt stated that Canadians were not granted anything higher than Top Secret. However, in the 1991 interview with Victorian, he contradicted this when asked if the Americans would have shared such "very secretive or above top secret" material. "They certainly would have," replied Solandt. "If we would have shown interest in it and the need to know. We have shared some above top secret information. This is not exactly what we regarded as being very important."

[3] Schwarz, Berthold "UFO Dynamics – Book 2" Carlstadt, New Jersey: Rainbow Books, 1983 p. 535

[4] Ibid. P. 534

[5] From the transcript of an interview between Wilbert Smith and Dr. Robert Sarbacher, September 15, 1950. Found in Wilbert Smith's personal files.

[6] E-mail "The Observer <pidivi@dsuper.net> to Grant Cameron"

[7] The Observer "Roswell is Factual" alt. Alien Visitors 06/18/1997

[8] Another thing that indicates the grey was foreign to Smith and everyone else in the 1950s was the reaction of Wilbert Smith's metallurgist to Dr. Robert Sarbacher's description of the alien bodies as "insect like." When this Sarbacher/Steinman letter became public I sent it to the metallurgist for comment. He phoned days later absolutely shocked at the insect description. He told me that the Smith group had discussed the aliens many times and that this type of alien was never brought up.

[9] Pope, Nick, "The Uninvited"

[10] Jacobs, David "The UFO Controversy In America" Indiana University Press 1975 p. 113.

FACTS ABOUT GRANT CAMERON

Grant Cameron is the recipient of the Leeds Conference International Researcher of the Year and the UFO Congress Researcher of the Year. He became involved in Ufology as the Vietnam War ended in May 1975 with personal sightings of a UFO-type object which locally became known as Charlie Red Star. A book titled, "Tales of Charlie Red Star" has been written about the phenomenon. These sightings led to a decade of research into the early work done by the Canadian government into the flying saucer phenomena. Cameron became the authority on the program and Wilbert B. Smith who headed it up. From here Cameron proceeded to do almost three decades of research into the role of the President of the United States in the UFO mystery. He is one of the foremost authorities on Hillary Clinton and Donald Trump and their UFO connection. Most of that research is found at the Presidents UFO Website – www.presidentialufo.com or in two recently released books "The Clinton UFO Storybook" and "Managing Magic: The Government's UFO Disclosure Plan."After experiencing a mental download event on February 26, 2012, Cameron turned his research interests away from "nuts and bolts" research to the role of consciousness in the UFO phenomena. This new research has expanded out to the possible involvement of extraterrestrials in modern music, and in the aspects of inspirations and downloads in science discoveries, inventions, Nobel Prizes, music, art, books, near death experiences, meditation, and with individuals known as savants and prodigies.Cameron has lectured widely in Canada, the United States and Europe. He was one of the 40 witnesses that testified in front of six ex-Senators and Congressmen in Washington for the "Citizen's Hearing on Disclosure." He has appeared on many television documentaries on UFOs, and been interviewed by nearly a hundred radio shows including a series of appearances on Coast to Coast AM.Cameron co-authored a book on the government UFO cover-up called "UFOs, Area-51, and the Government," and a book, "Alien Bedtime Stories" which contains 72 articles on UFOs as they relate to the Presidents, consciousness, abductions, and musicians. He has just released three other books related to consciousness called "Inspired: The Paranormal World of Creativity," "Tuned-In: The Creative World of Music," and "Managing Magic: The Government's UFO Disclosure Plan."

Web Sites:

www.presidentialufo.com
www.hillaryclintonufo.com
SUGGESTED READING

MANAGING MAGIC – THE GOVERNMENT DISCLOSURE PLAN

TALES OF CHARLIE RED STAR

UFOS, AREA 51 AND GOVERNMENT INFORMANTS

CANADA HUNTS FOR SAUCERS: DOZENS OF FLYING SAUCER REPORTS HAVE RESULTED IN THE CREATION OF A CANADIAN FLYING SAUCER OBSERVATORY

PROJECT MAGNET

Written by John C. Ross for "Fate Magazine" in 1954

In a tiny building only 12 feet square at Shirley's Bay, 10 miles north of Ottawa, is housed one of the most unusual collections of instruments ever crammed into so small a space. It is the world's first flying saucer observatory.

The sighting station went into operation with little fanfare. At first Canadian Government officials were inclined to dismiss the very existence of the station as a figment of the imagination. On the day before it opened, Dr. O. M. Solandt, chairman of the Defense Research Board, professed complete ignorance of the project. "Nothing to do with the Defense Research Board," he said.

"True enough," it turned out. The station was constructed by the National Research Council and officially announced by the Hon. Lionel Chevrier, Minister of Transport. Mr. Chevrier did not explain the denial of the project by Dr. Omond Solandt, who was quick to modify his statement, explaining only that his board was not involved in the project.

"However, we are continuing to study new reports (of flying saucers)," he admitted. "And are alert to the possibilities of discoveries of that nature."

Meanwhile, reports of new saucer sightings have been coming in from all over Canada.

In North Bay Ontario, The Daily Nugget has a file of 16 persons who have reported sightings of orange-colored discs. The newspaper says that all the accounts check closely in size, color, speed, and flying behavior.

One North Bay citizen late in October told of a dozen night sightings of a "funny orange globe" which came out of the northeastern skies, wandered back and forth across the sky, and then vanished.

In the fall of 1951, three persons reported a daytime sighting over Lake Nipissing. Each saw it from a different shore and did not know of the others' reports. Each reported a silver, round-shaped star going through strange maneuvers.

Orange-red discs have appeared over the Royal Canadians Air Force base at North Bay several times. Once such an object circled, dived and zigzagged over the field for eight minutes. Another time a disc approached from the southwest, stopped, hovered over the field, reversed direction, and disappeared in a

PROJECT MAGNET

climbing turn.

It is dozens of such reports that have resulted in the creation of Canada's flying saucers observatory – some call it a "disc watching" station. Management of the station is under the Canadian saucer project called "Project Magnet." Project Magnet was given formal recognition three years ago by the Department of Transport on an understanding that it was to be confined to the broadcast and measurement section of the telecommunications division of the department and that no appropriation of public funds be required for its support.

Actually Project Magnet was created to investigate the possibility of discs powered by magnetic propulsion.

Tremendously complex and expensive equipment has gone into the tiny building at Shirley's Bay. The equipment is designed to detect gamma rays, magnetic fluctuations, radio noises and gravity or mass changes in the atmosphere.

Installed in the tiny little structure is an ionospheric reactor to determine the height, pattern, and conduct of the ionized layers of gases several hundred miles in the atmosphere.

There is a new-type instrument called a gravimeter, imported from Sweden, to measure the earth's gravity; a magnetometer, to record the variations in the earth's magnetic field; a radio set running full volume at 530 kilocycles to pick up any radio noises; and a counter to detect atomic rays from the outer atmosphere.

Peter Dempson of the Telegram staff reports that all the instruments are connected with a control panel filled with lights, dials and other instruments, which record the individual findings on paper.

The station is not manned, but is connected directly by an alarm bell system with the nearby ionospheric station at Shirley's Bay, where a staff of telecommunication experts are on 24-hour duty.

Eventually, relays will carry the information recorded by the instruments in the sighting station to the main building. Any unusual variations in the information they provide will trigger the ionosphere recorder – an instrument that transmits a radio signal 250 miles into the sky. The signal bounces off the heavy layers in the ionosphere, and is reflected back to be picked up by a radar-like instrument. Officials believe that it would record any flying saucer in the area.

"If anything should happen, the findings of this recorder would prove very valuable," one official said.

The effective range of the other instruments is limited to about 50 miles.

Wilbert B. Smith, engineer-in-change of the project, believes that on the basis of past reports there is a 90 to 95 per cent probability that the sighted phenomena that the station was set up to observe actually do exist. Mr. Smith's official position is engineer in change of the telecommunications division of the Department of Transport. He and members on his staff have conducted saucer investigations for five years as a hobby and Project Magnet now represents the official Canadian Government's official seal of approval on their efforts. Smith, himself, believes that there is a 60 per cent probability that flying saucers are "alien vehicles."

Top Canadian scientists, including Dr. C. J. MacKenzie, former head of the National Research Council and the Canadian Atomic Energy Project, have consistently refused to ridicule any saucer reports.

"My own opinion is that the reports are valid," Smith told Gerald Waring, Canadian news writer. "The optical illusion explanation is lovely, but in every sighting there is always some factor which rules it out. So we've decided to learn just what flying saucers are."

Because of the comparatively large number of sightings in Canada, and despite the fact that most of his instruments have only a 50-mile range, Smith predicts that his instruments will report at least one saucer within a year. He points to a fact which may or may not be significant – that saucer sightings increase when the planet Mars is nearest to Earth. These close ranges occur every 26 months. Next summer the earth will come within 40 million miles of Mars, and in 1956 it will come within 35 million miles.

Others aiding engineer Smith include Dr. James Watt, theoretical physicist with the Research Board; John H. Thompson, technical information expert on telecommunications; Professor J. T. Wilson of the University of Toronto; and Dr. G. D. Garland, gravity specialist with Dominion Observatory.

The Shirley's Bay observatory had its first major test in January, just two months after it was established. A ball of fire flashed across Ontario, Quebec, and New York State in the early dawn and may have fallen into Georgian Bay. Startled residents of Ontario and Quebec started calling police and radio stations for an explanation. From Parry Sound, Ontario, came reports of an explosion "like a bomb."

The observatory was able to report that it was a meteor. Director Smith stated that the object was noted at the flying saucer station but failed to register on the delicate instruments, indicating that it definitely was not a saucer.

"Not a squiggle on our electronic devices," Smith said. "If it had been a saucer, our recorder would have shown it." Smith pointed out that his station's electronic devices would not detect meteors unless they were of "great mass" and passed very close.

This leaves no doubt whatever that the little building at Shirley's Bay was a flying saucer station only.

PROJECT MAGNET

INTRODUCTION
ORTHODOX SCIENCE & THEOLOGY TO BE REPLACED IN NEW AGE
By Dr. George Hunt Williamson

(Dr. Williamson is the well-known author of such books as ROAD IN THE SKY; THE SAUCERS SPEAK; UFOs CONFIDENTIAL; SECRET PLACES OF THE LION and OTHER TONGUES, OTHER FLESH.)

The word "orthodox" implies a standard of truth, so that conformity with it is right, and divergence from it error; but the standard itself may vary from age to age.

We can look back into history and see many examples of how orthodox views gave way to new knowledge. Most of these changes did not take place overnight. The example, well-known to every school child, is the story of Columbus and how the great scientists of his day called him a crazy fanatic for believing earth was round. This idea was not Columbus' own, for it had been circulated among the ancients for thousands of years; yet, the majority of the people in the world did not embrace this theory until only a few hundred years ago. In fact, there are still people today who believe Earth to be flat!

Many so-called prophets today are foretelling horrible destruction and doom for the people of Earth. They claim life is eternal, yet they fear the transition called "death." The space friends are here to help us, not to destroy us, and, although there are going to be vast changes taking place from time to time on the physical, mental and spiritual planes, still only the good is to be inherited by man on this sorrowful planet!

Earthman has reached the stage in his evolution where he must be shown that he is not merely a lonely accident on one world only. His brothers and sisters exist on literally billions and billions of worlds in the Omniverse! As we come more and more under the beneficent rays of Aquarius, cosmic-ray bombardment will become more intensified and EVERYTHING on our planet will be changed vibrationally.

For centuries, Theology has battled Science, and vice versa. What they are arguing about is not known, for the two are really one, and will become one in the "Golden Dawn" approaching rapidly. All former theories will be discarded—or at least improved upon. We will know definitely where we have been inaccurate in the past and why! Truth will not contradict Truth.

Therefore our Philosophy of Life will be built on a science that recognizes a Creator of the Cosmos and a Divine Plan working everywhere! No longer will we be required to follow certain ritualistic practices or believe certain dogma in order to get into "heaven." On the other hand, we will no longer have to swing to the other side of the road to embrace the cold, bare facts of materialistic science. In short, we are about to "level off" or "get in balance."

Matters are what they are because of certain unstable or unbalanced conditions on the earth planet. With the help of our space friends we are about to enter a "Golden Age," but it won't happen by the time you read this article. We are even now in transition and it won't be very long before those thought to be "psychic fanatics" will find they are no longer in the minority! Call this New Age a new dispensation, a Golden Dawn or Age, a new density or dimension or Aquarius – it really doesn't matter – the important thing is . . . IT IS HERE!

There is another battle going on, and that is the West Coast Cold-War of the "ETHERIANS" and the "MATERIALISTS." Actually, there is no point of argument, just as there isn't in the eternal science-versus-religion fracas.

If you will read the theories of these researchers, I'm certain you will see no contradiction, unless it lies in the terminology of these various groups of individuals! I think it all stems from our archaic idea of what the word "ether" or "etheria" means. Upon hearing these words, we immediately think of "nothingness," absence of all except thought, etc. Now we realize that space and ether are one and the same thing, and all of us, whether on earth or some other world, are inhabitants or occupants of this medium! Vibrations here or there may be different, but all beings are "solid" when in their own environment.

As I said in previous articles and books, LET'S FORGET DIFFERENCES (which really don't exist) AND WORK TOGETHER FOR ALL MEN EVERYWHERE! Yes, scientific and theological dogma will take a "death blow," but science itself and the belief in a Creator will go on to greater revelations in the "Golden Dawn." May our Infinite Father guide us always, and may we stand in His Light!

PROJECT MAGNET

FACTS ABOUT WILBERT ("WILBUR") B. SMITH
By Timothy Green Beckley

Wilbert Brockhouse Smith was born in Lethbridge, in the providence of Alberta, Canada, on the 17th of February, 1910. Early in life he displayed an eager interest in the nature of things and at the age of 15 wrote a treatise on the concept of perpetual motion. He was also the author of several scientific novels. After having obtained his B.Sc. and M.Sc. degrees in Electrical Engineering from the University of British Columbia, he joined the staff of radio station C.J.O.R., Vancouver, in 1935, where he remained for four years and became chief engineer. In 1939 he joined the Department of Transport of Canada, where he continued his work in the broadcasting field and deserved much credit in advancing the technical aspects of broadcasting in Canada.

He participated in the development of Frequency Modulation and television broadcasting agreements between Canada and the United States. During World War II he was responsible for the establishment of a network of ionospheric measurement stations throughout Canada. In 1957 he was appointed superintendent of Radio Regulations Engineering, responsible for the engineering aspects of all matters concerning the use of radio in Canada, including equipment standards and radio relay systems,

In December, 1950, following his request to the Department of Transport, Project Magnet was authorized and permission granted to make use of the Department's laboratory and field facilities, in a study of Unidentified Flying Objects and the physical principles which might be involved. Unfortunately, the program was plagued by well-meaning but misguided journalists, to an extent where those who were involved in the project, and the Department, found themselves in an embarrassing position. Project Magnet was therefore officially dropped in 1954 and continued to operate strictly as a private venture.

His interest in UFOs was but one aspect of his activities. Although a skeptic by nature, he welcomed new ideas and encouraged their discussion. His investigations carried him into the fields of physics, philosophy and religion. As an engineer, he was foremost in his field and the holder of several patents. He undertook a thorough study of gravity and devised several gravity control experiments which produced limited but encouraging results. His correspondence was voluminous. The depth of his insight was well-reflected in both his correspondence and his conversation, and he was known for his ability to express himself clearly and convincingly on a wide variety of subjects, both orthodox and unorthodox.

In June 1942 Wilbert married Murl James. They took up residence at 10 Lotta Street, City View, on the outskirts of Ottawa, in 1950, where Murl still lives with their three children.

The last ten years of Wilbert's life were devoted to intensive thought and study. Several of his ideas he formulated into a manuscript entitled "The New Science."

As will be known to many readers, it was discovered in May of 1962 that Wilbert Smith was afflicted with cancer and after a valiant struggle, he died on December 27, 1962, at the age of 52.

Timothy Green Beckley

PROJECT MAGNET

THE SPACE BROTHERS' PHILOSOPHY AND WILBERT B. SMITH
By the Editors of TOPSIDE

Since the passing of our founder and the original editor of TOPSIDE, the late Wilbert B. Smith, in December, 1962, it has been part of the editorial policy of TOPSIDE to pass on to its readers messages purporting to come from the Space Brothers as received through contacts established by WBS during his lifetime on Earth and to maintain his scientific approach in the method of obtaining these messages, i.e., for each message or statement received, further confirmation is sought from two other independent sources via a network of telepathic contactees across the world, and it is interesting to note that frequently some of these so-called "contactees" are unaware that they are acting in this capacity and proffer the necessary confirmation unasked.

The Space Brothers often work this way, using any sincere, receptive channel through whom to pass on valuable information. Any dedicated UFO worker may be assured that his or her services, either consciously or unconsciously, are being effectively used by those of the space people concerned with the welfare of their Earth Brother, as part of the Great Plan to enlighten mankind on Earth and prepare it for the wider horizons of the New Age. This statement is part of the Space Brothers Philosophy as received by Wilbert B. Smith.

In recent years, there have appeared in print a couple of articles questioning the validity of WBS's claims. One of these appeared in the July-August 1966 issue of "Flying Saucer Review" which, based on an evasive reply received from a Canadian Government Department, cast doubts on the UFO research work conducted by WBS in the Canadian Government's "Project Magnet," set up at Shirley's Bay, near Ottawa, in December 1950, and officially closed in October, 1954. In fairness to "Flying Saucer Review," it must be added that an appeal was made for a refutation or clarification of these doubts from Canada, but, at that time, for a very valid reason, we (mainly government employees) were not in a position to provide this, even though we had the evidence to substantiate WBS's statements.

The other article was one that appeared in the Canadian syndicated publication, "Week-End Magazine", of Nov. 12, 1966, in which the intended slur of "Spiritualism" was flung at WBS's contacts with the space people and TOPSIDE was accused of "reflecting his interest in the occult." It will be noted from the dates that these two courageous writers (who shall remain nameless here) and their supporting government quotees, waited until WBS was no longer around to defend his good name, but this, alas, has ever been the lot of men with ideas and concepts in advance of their time who dared to "rock the boat" of the Establishment.

Hitherto, we had decided to treat these disparaging remarks with the silent contempt they deserved, believing (a) that they emanated from unenlightened men not in possession of the full facts or were quoted by government officials who, with perhaps an understandable eye on their positions, decided to "play it safe" by following the government "party line" of the UFO policy of that time; and (b) that Wilbert Smith's established record as a senior government official, i.e., Chief of Telecommunications and Electronics Branch, Department of Transport, his distinguished career, with awards and honors, in the field of Technical Aspects of Broadcasting (including the development of Frequency Modulation and television broadcasting agreements between Canada and the U.S.A.), his scientific work as an inventor and holder of several patents, and above all, his high reputation as a man of complete sincerity and integrity, would stand on their own merits.

However, in view of the fact that an oblique challenge has been thrown at us in print, questioning "our guts to speak out in defense of Wilbert Smith," we think the time has come for a little plain speaking. In this regard, we refer to an article entitled "In Defense of Wilbert Smith" written by our esteemed UFO colleague, Ronald Caswell, Director of IGAP-Great Britain, which appeared in the December, 1967, issue of "UFO Contact." In fairness to the ONSC, it should be pointed out that Ron Caswell, writing from England, has been in a much better position to speak out openly than we, working for the Government of Canada in Ottawa, have been. He is also very well qualified to do so because during his three-year residence in Canada in the 1950s, he was a close associate of WBS and exchanged considerable correspondence with him. Extracts from this correspondence and some hitherto unpublished material concerning WBS appear in his article, which is informative, well-written, well-presented – and it pulls no punches.

For our part, we are prepared to support Ronald Caswell's Defense of Wilbert Smith, with the following remarks. With regard to the doubts expressed on WBS's UFO role in Project Magnet, with the Canadian Government's recent pronouncement confirming this, a barrier has been removed to our speaking more openly on this matter. As reported in the July, 1967 issue of TOPSIDE, the Canadian Government (with what appeared to be a change in its UFO policy) released to the press, through one of its Cabinet Ministers, the Hon. Paul Hellyer (at that time, Minister of Defense), details of a hitherto secret UFO project, namely the establishment of a UFO landing site at its Defense Research Board Experimental Station in Suffield, Alberta, making mention of an earlier special scientific committee set up in Canada to investigate UFOs, of which WBS was a member. It was further stated that as a part of Project Magnet, WBS set up specially designed apparatus detecting UFOs passing overhead. This official statement, we consider, should effectively silence the "Doubting Thomases" who attempted to discredit WBS's UFO research work in this government project, once and for all. We may add that evidence exists of the official closing-down of the UFO side of Project Magnet, after which WBS continued this work on a private basis, with permission to use government laboratory facilities, etc., on his own time and at no cost to the Treasury.

As for the charge of "Spiritualism," this, of course, is a lot of nonsense, and it is somewhat amusing to observe the way in which some scientists, whose closed minds cannot grasp anything beyond their measurable five senses, use this expression almost as if it were a dirty word! Like WBS, we in the Ottawa New Sciences Club endeavor to keep an open mind on all subjects and therefore we do not deny whatever truth there may be in Spiritualism, but the fact remains that we are not and never have been practicing spiritualists or occultists. Let it therefore be categorically stated that Wilbert Smith, first and foremost a scientist, never dabbled in spiritualist activities; his profound study of the UFO Mystery led him inevitably to the Science of Metaphysics at which, having an open mind eager to learn all truths, he became an Advanced Adept, and it was by this means that he secured invaluable scientific and philosophic data from the Space Brothers, always using the scientific method of independent confirmation of information received, as described earlier.

These messages were received by a specially selected intermediary through direct telepathic communication with the Space Brothers and, since mental telepathy and ESP are now accepted facts by many earth scientists who have made a serious study of these phenomena, it should not be too difficult for skeptics to accept that, if thought transference is possible at great distance on this planet, then the exchange of pure thought between any intelligent beings must be equally possible throughout the wider distance of Outer Space. Natural Laws of the Cosmos are not confined to this planet alone.

In regard to the scientific data WBS obtained from his space friends, "The Boys from Topside," he was able to test their genuineness and practical workability by protracted tests and experiments in the laboratory, and in this connection it should be pointed out that since it is against the Cosmic Laws of the Space Brothers to drop unearned answers to scientific questions into the laps of earth scientists, all that WBS received from them were certain guidelines or suggested avenues of research for him to explore and the actual work of finding the answers to scientific problems was left to WBS to fathom out. Always, the Space Brothers were helpful, quick to point out when he was on the wrong track, and offering further suggestions of approach to the solution of a problem; but never once did they spell out the complete answer. This would have been contrary to the Universal Law that there is no virtue or merit to anything that is not achieved by personal effort. However, by diligent research and many experiments on a trial or error basis, WBS eventually proved much of the truth of the scientific data conveyed to him by the Space Brothers, and unique inventions resulted.

Some of these devices, thoroughly tested and proved accurate in results by WBS and his group, have regrettably remained unacceptable to Earth scientists because of their unorthodox origin, but the day may yet dawn when they will be used for the benefit of humanity. It may interest our readers to learn that the specially-selected contactee used by the Space Brothers to pass on purely scientific data for WBS invariably found this information completely unintelligible – but it proved most pertinent to and was clearly understood by WBS. It is a strange fact, but since the passing of WBS, this particular channel has never been used again, which would seem to indicate proof-positive of the genuineness of the contact. Conversely, the contactee channels supplying information on the Space Brothers' Philosophy remain open to us and serve as proof that we still have a job to do. Our space friends are wonderfully logical!

We would reiterate then, that WBS was not a spiritualist in the sense interpreted by the vast masses. He was a pioneer scientist, perhaps in advance of his Age, an indefatigable searcher for advanced scientific truths – and he was too intelligent a man to seek such truths by communication with the so-called "dead," whose knowledge of such matters might conceivably be less than his own. With the advent of increased UFO activity around this planet in the 1950s, WBS, at first an extreme skeptic, made an intensive study of the mystery and finally became convinced of the reality of extraterrestrials visiting earth in spacecraft of superior technology, capable of performing feats which defied our present knowledge of physics. Unable to find the answer to the mystery on the physical plane, he was led to the Science of Metaphysics which, in turn, led to direct communication with the Space Brothers and knowledge of their Philosophy, and there, to quote his own words, "was the answer in all its grandeur!"

We feel it safe to predict that, in the annals of recent UFO history, Wilbert B. Smith's name will remain untarnished as a man of great integrity, as an early world pioneer of the truth of the UFOs, who, particularly in those early years of ridicule and scorn, had the bold courage of his own convictions and who tackled the Biggest Enigma of the Century with a purely scientific approach.

PROJECT MAGNET

THE REALITY OF SPACECRAFT

EDITOR'S NOTE: The following chapters written by Wilbert B. Smith during his leadership of the Ottawa New Sciences Club express many of his views on the subjects of Flying Saucers, Life on Other Planets, Canada's Project Magnet, and the philosophy of the Space Brothers.

*****

I have been actively engaged in the investigation of the group phenomena known as flying saucers for several years. During this period I have read most of the available literature on the subject, interviewed a great many people who have seen unusual things in the sky, examined many pictures and physical objects, made observations with scientific instruments and carried on a series of communications with intelligences claiming to be extraterrestrial.

I began the investigations out of curiosity and as an extreme skeptic, fully expecting to find the phenomena to be due to man-made or natural causes. I am 48 years old, hold a Master's Degree in Electrical Engineering, occupy a responsible position in the Canadian Government, hold a half dozen patents, am author of several technical papers, and in general enjoy a background in technical work and science indicating at least an average competence to study and report on phenomena of a scientific nature. I have tried so far as possible to use conventional and standard methods and equipment to investigate all possible angles before drawing any conclusions. In other words, I have followed the same general procedures which I would have followed if I had undertaken to study some more prosaic subject, such as radio wave propagation.

The first phase of the work consisted of reading all available literature, collecting as much observational data as possible, and in general getting a fair perspective of the problem. The second phase involved theoretical and laboratory work to find openings in our technology and to establish relevant reference points, and the third phase involved following up the many and varied leads which developed from the first two phases.

I do not intend to dwell on the first phase of this work as my experience was quite parallel with that of other investigators who have provided extensive published reports of their findings. Nor will I dwell on the many dead ends which were explored which looked promising at first but faded out under careful investigation. Nor will I be able to be as specific as I would like to be with respect to material given to me in confidence or which came to me through "classified" channels. Furthermore, it is not my intention to try and convert anyone to my way of thinking but merely to state what I believe and why I believe it.

Let us look at a few facts.

(1) Hundreds of normal honest people have seen lights in the sky which behaved like no light normally seen in the sky ought to behave.

(2) Hundreds of normal honest people have seen what appear to be solid real objects in the sky which behaved like no object normally seen in the sky ought to behave.

(3) Hundreds of people have seen objects in Earth's atmosphere at sufficiently close range to see enough detail to enable them to say definitely what the objects were not, even though they could not identify what they were.

(4) Descriptions of these objects, from observers where circumstances virtually preclude collusion, check quite well among themselves and against data received from other sources.

It is not reasonable to assume that hundreds of ordinary normal people whose word we would readily accept under more mundane circumstances, for instance as witnesses to an automobile accident, should suddenly become liars, fools, neurotics, and otherwise quite incompetent observers. I have interviewed many of these people myself and I am convinced that they are sane, sober, honest folk who are reporting as best they can something which they really did witness. I will concede that maybe some of these people did not do as good a job of observing as someone who was better trained might have done, but within their limits I believe they did honestly report what they saw.

Let us look at a few more facts.

(1) There have been several close brushes with these objects and in one case at least the aircraft pilot lost his life as a consequence. (Capt. Thomas Mantell was reported killed as a result of chasing a flying saucer on January 7, 1947).

(2) People who have been near these objects have described physical sensations which are unusual to say the least, but which are quite consistent with what is known of the technology under which they operate.

While the foregoing may seem rather incredible, nevertheless there exist quite good records in support of these occurrences. Furthermore, the technology of which we have been able to get a glimpse, namely that of manipulation of the three basic fields, electric, magnet and tempic, indicates quite a straightforward answer to an explanation of these phenomena. In Mantell's case the altered field configuration in the vicinity of the craft reduced the binding forces within the structural members of the aircraft to a value below that of the load which they were expected to carry, so they just came apart. These altered binding forces have been measured by simple instruments by people in my group and have been found to be quite significant. Furthermore, there was probably a substantial reduction in tempic field intensity in the vicinity of the craft which Mantell approached, which would result in an effective rise in temperature of the aircraft and contents. I understand Mantell's body gave every indication of having been subjected to considerable heat, and not from the outside in.

There have been quite a number of alleged communications with intelligences claiming to be extraterrestrial. I have followed up each such instance which came to my attention to the best of my ability in an effort to (a) establish or disprove the validity of the alleged communication, and (b) to obtain any information which might be available if the contact should prove to be authentic.

As might be expected, many of the contacts provided little or nothing of value, but a few did pay off. Some of the contacts have been the subject of published material, but by far the majority are confidential; and there are a surprising number of these contacts.

The procedure in checking contacts was to ask a number of innocuous but significant questions and compare the answers with the answers to the same questions as obtained through other contacts. Questions were of the type: Do people live on the planet Mars? If so, what is the general shape of their houses? Do people on Mars use coinage money? If so, what does it look like? All together some hundred or more questions were involved. The results were spectacular to say the least. Among the contacts that might be classed as authentic there was almost complete agreement. Among the other alleged contacts there was extremely poor agreement, or none at all, of course, where agreement was general, but one or two points didn't fit in, an effort was made to find out the reason for the discrepancy. In each case it was found that someone had injected a terrestrial idea or comment, frequently of a religious nature, instead of transmitting faithfully that which was received.

Having located what seemed to be channels of communication between ourselves and these extraterrestrial intelligences, the next and obvious step was to try and get as much information as possible. As may be expected, this effort was at first directed toward science and technology, but it soon became apparent that there was a very real and quite large gap between this alien science and that in which I had been trained. Certain crucial experiments were suggested and carried out, and in each case the results confirmed the validity of the alien science.

Beyond this point the alien science just seemed to be incomprehensible.

There followed a period of soul searching during which many doubts were raised. We felt that we had established the reality of the craft from elsewhere, and of the intelligences associated with them, and while we were able to establish that these people all told the same story, was that story the truth? There existed some pretty good evidence to support their statements, and precious little with which to disprove them, but we did not overlook the possibility that there might be some other more conventional explanation.

We looked carefully at every conventional explanation we could find, but they all fell quite short of the mark. If the whole thing were a delusion, then quite a large number of people must be suffering from the same delusion, and an externalized delusion into the bargain. If it were a hoax, then it was by far the most gigantic hoax the world had ever known, and to what end, and by whom perpetrated, and who was putting up the money, because some of the "evidence" must have cost a pretty penny to produce. The inevitable conclusion was that it was all real enough, and that these people from elsewhere were probably just what they claimed to be. The science however was definitely alien and possibly forever beyond our comprehension. So another approach was tried, the philosophical, and here the answer was found in all its grandeur!

The people from elsewhere displayed great patience and understanding in helping me to overcome many of the prejudices and stores of misinformation which I had spent many years accumulating. I began for the first time in my life to realize the basic ONENESS of the Universe and all that is in it.

Science, philosophy, religion, substance, and energy are all facets of the same jewel, and before any one facet of the jewel can really be appreciated, the form of the jewel itself must be perceived. One of the most important things I had to realize was that we are not alone. The human race in the form of MAN extends throughout the Universe and is incredibly ancient. Also, its appearance in physical form is but one of its many manifestations along the path of progress. Our civilization here on earth is only one of the many that have come and gone. This planet has been colonized many times by people from elsewhere, and our present human race are blood brothers of these people. Is it any wonder that they are interested in us? To orthodox thinkers this may seem strange, but not nearly as strange as our ideas on evolution!

The question might be asked, "If these people really are our brothers and are interested in our welfare, why do they remain so aloof?" We have been given the answer. There is a basic law of the universe which grants each and every individual independence and freedom of choice, so that he may experience and learn from his experiences. No one has the right to interfere in the affairs of others. In fact, our Ten Commandments are directives against interference. If we disregard this law we must suffer the consequences, and a little thought will show that the present deplorable world state is directly attributable to violation of this principle.

These people from elsewhere have much greater knowledge than we have regarding the sequences which must not be altered, and while they may have every desire in the world to help us, they may not do so at this time without running the risk of altering significantly sequences which are very necessary to our development. Therefore, while they stand by ready, able and willing to help us, they may not do so until a propitious time of which they will be informed in due course. The dividing line between help and interference is very delicate indeed and sometimes hard to perceive, but it is a mark of individual and collective progress how well we can be guided by it.

I am told that one of our difficulties is that we do not recognize a sufficient number of dimensions and make use of them in our science. Furthermore, we do not recognize the true nature of dimensions or their place in the universe. I am told that so far as we are concerned there are twelve dimensions, and these provide the necessary and sufficient structure for the entire universe. Our concepts of dimensions are most inadequate and restrictive, and so long as we persist in them we can never transcend the world of mechanical processes which we have conjured up.

In science we have an established procedure always to tie a new theory or discovery or observation to that which we already know, even though to do so requires extensive "patchwork" and "perturbation" factors to be applied to our existing knowledge to make the new knowledge fit. We invariably assume that the new knowledge must somehow be closely related to the old and we are most zealous in tying the two together. As a consequence we bend and warp our units of knowledge so that we can fasten them together whether or not they belong together, until we have fabricated quite a structure which is almost completely closed on itself. Consequently, when we do find knowledge which should, but just won't, fit our structure, we don't quite know what to do with it, so we usually reject it.

I am informed that science is really much more simple than we imagine, and all the component parts fit together perfectly without any corrections. Possibly, we should start over again and reassemble our knowledge in a different pattern, and this time fit the pieces of the jigsaw puzzle together properly without trimming the pieces. I feel sure that were we to do this, and accept the philosophy upon which this new approach must of necessity be based, we will be able to enjoy the technology and the way of life which is demonstrated to us by the presence of the spacecraft and our brothers from elsewhere.

PROJECT MAGNET

WE ARE NOT ALONE

Our universe is a very large place, much larger than our minds are capable of understanding. There are several billions of stars in our own Milky Way alone, and there are billions of similar galaxies scattered throughout space and within range of our large telescopes. The universe is also incredibly old. Our Earth alone is estimated to be several billion years old, and it is presumed that the stars are much older. Maybe the universe doesn't even have an age; perhaps it is eternal and ever passing through the cycle of energy to matter and matter to energy. The episode of Man on this planet, so far as we can determine, is relatively an extremely small portion of the larger time that the universe has existed, and the period of recorded history is relatively even shorter.

We consider the race of Man to be native to this planet and to have evolved here from lower life forms. We look upon our present civilization with pride and realize that we have accomplished much, particularly in the last few centuries. Even in the past few decades we have made tremendous progress in certain directions. Therefore, it is only natural that we should be egotistical about our position in the universe. But are we alone? Are there not others in the universe who, also, have progressed? The universe is very large and has been here a long time.

In the past few years we have taken our first faltering steps out into the vastness of space, first through the Sputniks and now through manned space flight. There is no doubt that we can do it, and if we can refrain from blowing ourselves to glory with atom bombs, we most certainly will do it. In the light of our present technology, and not allowing for any basic new discoveries, our timetable calls for interplanetary space travel well before the year 2000 and a good possibility of interstellar trips being initiated shortly thereafter.

Our space travel plans include exploration, exploitation and colonization of the other planets, so far as this may be possible, and there is no doubt that this thinking will be extended to the planets attached to other stars as soon as we can arrange to get there. Mankind has always been an adventuresome creature, exploring, conquering, colonizing and exploiting, and there is little reason to think that his future actions will be much different from those in his past.

Our large telescopes indicate low order perturbations in the positions of several of the nearer stars, such as could be accounted for by the presence of large planets, and if there are large ones there will probably be smaller ones also. In fact, it is generally agreed now that planets attached to stars are more probably the rule than the exception, and that we will eventually find the heavens filled with all sorts of primary and secondary bodies.

When we consider the extent, the age, and the opportunity of the universe, and the fact that we do have intelligent life here on this planet, it is only reasonable to speculate that somewhere else in the universe and the eternity of time, other intelligent life could have blossomed forth. Since we have made such rapid progress toward space travel in such a short time, a differential of only a few hundred or at the most a few thousand years between the development on some other planet and ours could easily have resulted in a race capable of doing right now what we plan to do in the near future. Furthermore, it is quite possible that such a race may have reached this critical point eons ago, and to them space travel is as commonplace as the wheeled vehicle is to us.

Now, if this should be the case, and this alien race were anything like us, they would probably set forth to explore and colonize as rapidly as their means would permit. It is rather obvious that, even with the speeds of travel available to us, it would be much quicker to colonize the universe than to wait for Nature to evolve separate races in each and every favorable environment. In fact, intelligent races might even set about accelerating environmental conditions to their liking, seeding and stocking planets with appropriate life forms, and watching over them while they develop.

The foregoing is not just idle speculation, since we have a great deal of evidence that something like this is actually happening. The Darwinian theory of evolution shows certain relationships between the various life forms which inhabit this planet, but there is very little evidence to indicate that they all evolved here. Maybe some of them did, but a more reasonable explanation is that they were brought here when the planet was in suitable condition to receive them. Recent spectroscopic observations of the reflected light from Mars shows the presence of vegetation which synthesizes sugar, thus making it closely related to much terrestrial vegetation. Radio telescopes are picking up all sorts of radio noises from the sky, many of which are so systematic as to preclude natural origin. Peculiar markings, light flashes, and cloud or dust formations have been seen on Mars and our moon. And, most significant of all, the craft of these alien beings have been seen near, and on, earth!

Legends and history abound in stories of visits to earth by beings from the sky; beings which came in strange craft capable of the most extraordinary performance, and who themselves possessed great powers or had at their command strange forces, much beyond the understanding of the simple folk who witnessed these things. There is much evidence that this has gone on all through the ages, and is going on right now. With excellent news gathering and disseminating means at our disposal, very little happens anywhere in the world which is not reported, and, if it is of sufficient interest, gets wide publicity. During the last ten years or more there has been much publicity about flying saucers and thousands of reports have been made of sightings of these strange objects in our skies. But this is not an exclusively recent phenomenon; only the publicity is recent. Ever since we have had newspapers there have been similar reports, but the absence of news services until recent times usually confined the details to a few local papers, and searches of old newspaper files confirm that flying saucers are old stuff.

The tense international situation in recent years has made everyone jittery and anything in the skies which could not be established as known and friendly was regarded with suspicion. Consequently, procedures, projects, and publicity combined to make the whole subject of flying saucers appear quite out of perspective. Instead of recognizing them for what they probably really were, they became a ward of the military, and since the military are charged only with the defense of a country, their interests waned when they had established the fact that the saucers apparently were not hostile. But in order to arrive at this conclusion they collected much data, classified it, and buried it so effectively that no one else could get at it, and those who might have been able to sort the matter out found themselves deprived of the basic data and had to content themselves with the bit which escaped the clutches of the military. However, on the basis of this material, some rather startling conclusions have been reached.

Thousands of people have seen lights and apparently solid objects in the sky which behave as no light or object normally seen in the sky ought to behave. Thousands have seen these objects under circumstances which enabled them to say definitely what they were not, even though they were unable to say what they were. Reliable photographs and movies have been taken, and bits of "hardware" collected which cannot be explained away without challenging the integrity of many witnesses. Simultaneous visual sightings and radar fixes exist in a great many cases, and there is quite a bit of evidence of physical contact with these strange craft.

In several instances reliable people have reported seeing the beings who ride about on these craft, and they say they look just like us. There are quite a number of reported contacts between these people from elsewhere and people of earth, and although this latter point may be hard to prove it is equally hard to disprove, and the results of these contacts are remarkably consistent and enlightening. At the present time there are quite a number of books, magazines and bulletins devoted to the study of flying saucers, and anyone who wishes to establish for himself the validity of these things will find no dearth of material.

At this point we may summarize the position somewhat as follows: There is virtually no doubt that alien craft are visiting Earth, and that the beings who operate them are very much like us, probably our distant relatives.

Considering the age and extent of the universe, it is reasonable that space travel, exploration and colonization, may be quite commonplace among races of mankind more advanced than we are. Information obtained through alleged "contacts" confirm the general nature of the picture as presented herewith, together with quite a bit of interesting side-lighting on the technology, customs, way-of-life, and philosophy of these people from elsewhere. It would appear that we are well along the way to becoming truly civilized, and if we can refrain from committing racial suicide and learn to respect the dignity, divinity and brotherhood of man, we can expect eventually to be welcomed into the great cosmic fraternity of advanced races that inhabit the regions beyond the limits of this little planet.

PROJECT MAGNET

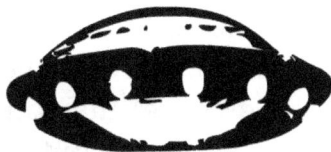

SPUTNIKS, SAUCERS AND SPACECRAFT

This section consists of a paper which was given to the Illuminating Engineering Society, Canadian Regional Conference, at a luncheon on June 11, 1959, in Ottawa.

On October 3, 1957, the Russians astonished the world by placing an artificial satellite called Sputnik in orbit around Earth. To most of the world, artificial satellites were things which might happen sometime in the dim and distant future, but to have a satellite actually aloft brought home the fact that space travel was about to become a reality. There were official announcements that Sputnik was there and many people managed to get glimpses of it as it raced across the sky. Because it was announced officially, it was considered quite proper for people to admit having seen it.

With an artificial satellite aloft and people looking skyward, there was an increasing number of reports of objects being seen which were not Sputniks. Many of these objects were confused with the Sputniks and this confusion would have persisted except for the fact that the Sputnik orbit was known and predictable. Many of these objects were recognized by their viewers as definitely not Sputniks, and since it was now considered polite to admit having seen things in the sky, many of these reports came forward and were added to the already thick files of flying saucer sightings.

The fact of the first Sputnik, and the many more which followed, made it quite apparent that our race was upon the threshold of space travel, and had actually taken the first step into the great outside. With this realization came also the realization that space travel was not really quite as fantastic as it had seemed at first, and that it was quite within the realm of possibility that some other race elsewhere might be a bit ahead of us and actually be doing it, and that maybe there was something to all the stories about the flying saucers after all. However, officialdom was not yet quite ready to admit the reality of the saucers, probably because they were not yet ready with all the answers to the questions which would be asked.

During the past ten years I have made a serious and extensive study of the

49

phenomenon of flying saucers. I have covered every aspect that I could come to grips with, and have arrived at some conclusions which, I might say, are entirely my own and do not represent any views which might be held officially or unofficially by the Canadian government. I think that many of these objects are spacecraft, and that they come from "elsewhere" than on this planet; that they are built and operated by beings very much like us, but who are more advanced in the business of living than we are; and that the saucers represent a technology which is much ahead of ours. I do not propose to wade through the reams of material upon which these conclusions are based, since this is practically all available in the current literature; I propose only to summarize this material.

Many thousands of people have seen lights in the sky which behaved as no light normally seen in the sky ought to behave. Many thousands of people have seen what appear to be solid objects in the sky which behaved as no solid object normally seen in the sky ought to behave. Many people have seen objects at close enough range to be able to say definitely what these objects were not, even though they could not say what they were. Many scientific observations and pictures exist with respect to these objects which just can't be explained away without challenging the honesty of the observers.

I have interviewed many people who claimed to have seen a flying saucer, and I am convinced that they are normal honest folk who are reporting as best they can something which they actually did witness. We would be happy to accept the statements of these same people in a court of law as witnesses to something more mundane, such as an automobile accident, so why should we doubt them when they tell about having seen a flying saucer?

I do not think that these people are liars, fools, neurotics and hoaxers. Even if the sighting evidence were all we had, I would still be inclined to accept it as fairly well establishing the reality of spacecraft from elsewhere. However, we have in addition to visual evidence a variety of confirmation in other forms. Many sightings have been confirmed by radar with identical positions being established. Physical evidence of witnessed landings, such as imprints in soft ground, broken bushes, withered vegetation, etc., is plentiful and well-confirmed. Various items of "hardware" are known to exist, but are usually promptly clapped into security and therefore are not available to the general public. Substances such as "angel hair" and molten tin, etc., have been observed to drop from these craft, and have been gathered up and analyzed. Strong magnetic disturbances have been observed in the vicinity of these craft. In fact, I would say that many more people have more evidence supporting the reality of flying saucers than evidence for the reality of atom bombs. But atom bombs bear the stamp of official disclosure.

It is a well-known fact that our science consists of a few basic facts and a large amount of conjecture, cemented together with great numbers of "correction factors" and "perturbation factors." We have many anomalies in our science, but instead of heeding them as Nature's warning that there was something wrong with our concepts, we shoved them into the background and turned our thoughts to those things which appeared to be more self-consistent. Consequently, I am convinced, we have missed the boat on many occasions, and now when we have before us the magnificent fact that space travel through other means than on the business end of a rocket is possible, we are unable to cope with the situation, and instead of learning from these beings who come to us from elsewhere in flying saucers, we deny them, ignore them, and hope that they will go away.

I think that there is too much evidence to ignore that the saucers are real and are extraterrestrial spacecraft, and since their behavior cannot adequately be explained by our science, we are forced to the conclusion that this alien science transcends ours, and may even be beyond our reach.

Fortunately, a few serious investigators had the moral courage to face up to this problem in spite of the cries of "heresy" from orthodox science, and reasoned that if some other race could do these things, so could we. I will not dwell on the many dead ends which were investigated or the theories which were developed and discarded, because this is typical of any and all scientific progress. It is sufficient to say that many of our basic physical concepts were tested and found to be valid only under specific conditions, or are special cases of a more general concept. My own group has concentrated on problems associated with gravity, refusing to believe that Newton's Law ("every particle in the universe attracts every other particle with a force˜ which is equal to the product of the two masses and a universal gravitational constant divided by the square of the distance between the two masses") was the alpha and omega of gravity. Since flying saucers demonstrated what appeared to be gravity control, it certainly seemed logical to assume that such control could be established. Furthermore, certain aspects of the behavior of these craft gave us valuable clues to the real nature of the universe, and its elegant simplicity.

At the present time we do not have all the answers. Nor do we have anything like an integrated theory. All we have is a collection of facts based on observation and the results of a number of experiments, but we feel that this foundation is considerably more secure than that of our current orthodox science, for in it there are no anomalies. We know that gravity is not all what Newton visualized. Far from being a basic force in Nature, it is really a derived function, and is the consequence of a dynamic condition, not a static one. We know what goes into its makeup; we know its formula and we have a pretty good idea of how to go about bringing it under control.

We have conducted experiments that show that it is possible to create artificial gravity (not centrifugal force) and to alter the gravitational field of the earth.

PROJECT MAGNET

This we have done. It is fact. The next stop is to learn the rules and do the engineering necessary to convert a principle into workable hardware.

So far, this work on gravity has been carried on entirely as a personal project, privately financed at a cost which is minute compared with the cost of the current rocket program, and with the volunteer assistance of a few people who are sincerely interested enough to put in long hours after their normal working day, and face the criticism levelled at anyone who dares to think differently. I am sure that if even a small fraction of the money being spent on rockets were spent on proper research looking toward gravity control, with the example of the flying saucers before us, and with the possible help from those people from elsewhere, we could join them in space much sooner, more safely, and more economically than we will ever be able to do on the business end of a rocket.

PROJECT MAGNET

THE PHILOSOPHY OF THE SAUCERS

Possibly one of the most interesting aspects of the study of flying saucers, beyond the realization that they are real and extraterrestrial, is their philosophy. What manner of creatures build and fly them? What do they look like? How do they think? Are their ideas and ideals similar to ours? Could we understand them? All these and many other questions plague the serious investigator.

If we are to rely on sighting data alone we are bound to get a rather one-sided idea of these creatures. For example, we see saucers travelling at terrific speeds and then suddenly stop or change direction. Under our concepts of physics, no creature of flesh, blood and bone could withstand the terrific forces which would be associated with such actions. Therefore, we are likely to assume that the Saucerians must be either some manner of robot or a creature the like of which we have never encountered.

Again, it is hard to understand why any race of creatures having the tremendous power at their disposal which we see demonstrated by the saucers, should be content to fly rather aimlessly over our globe, without doing something more definite. If the tables were reversed, we most certainly would. After a very brief reconnaissance, we would land and announce to the natives that we were taking over. The fact that the Saucerians have made no such move appears to indicate that they must regard us in the same general category as the other flora and fauna native to this planet, and to them our civilization is so primitive as to be indistinguishable from that of the lower animals and insects.

We could go on speculating in this manner for quite a while without coming anywhere near the truth. Fortunately the people who come to us from elsewhere in flying saucers have seen fit to make contact with people of Earth, and to impart as much information and understanding as the contacts were capable of assimilating or passing along to others. There have been many published instances of contacts between these people from outside and people of earth, and a very great many more which have not been published.

As is always the case in any new and romantic field, there are those who exaggerate, but it is not too difficult to establish that the vast majority are honest and authentic. For instance, when a dozen or so independent contacts having no common connection, and each alone believing that he or she has been favored above all others to receive this message, all tell the same message, even to names and descriptions which tally perfectly, one has little choice but to believe that they are telling the truth.

Furthermore, when the material given to us through the many channels is all assembled and analyzed, it adds up to a complete and elegant philosophy which makes our efforts sound like the beating of jungle drums. These people tell us of a magnificent cosmic plan, of which we are a part, which transcends the lifetime of a single person or a nation, or a civilization, or even a planet or solar system. We are not merely told that there is something beyond our immediate experience; we are told what it is, why it is, and our relation thereto. Many of our most vexing problems are solved with a few words; at least we are told of the solutions if we have the understanding and fortitude to apply them. We are told of the inadequacies of our sciences and we have been given the basic grounding for a new science which is at once simpler and yet more embracing than the mathematical monstrosity which we have conjured up. We have been told of a way of life which is utopian beyond our dreams, and the means of attaining it. Can it be that such a self-consistent, magnificent philosophy is the figment of the imaginations of a number of misguided morons? I do not think so.

If the only evidence we had was philosophical, we might justifiably suspect it, but when coupled with the reality of the observations, thousands of them, we cannot dismiss it so easily. This is especially true when we consider that the science which has been passed to us from these people from elsewhere explains in a manner which we have been quite unable to do why the saucers behave as they do, and how it is that they can do things which to us are virtually impossible. The science and performance check perfectly!

Again, we have been told where our scientific ideas are wrong, or inadequate, and experiments have been suggested and carried out, and in every case the alien science has been vindicated. We may ask, if all this is known, why has it not been publicized, why are not these matters being studied instead of atom bombs? The answer: it has been publicized. Books have been written and hundreds and thousands of copies sold. There are available many periodicals containing this material which may be had for quite a nominal sum. Reports have been prepared by serious investigators and presented "through the proper channels." But it is truly said that one can lead a horse to water but one cannot make him drink!

Those who are in control of our society are satisfied with it the way it is and will resist any attempt to change anything which is likely to disturb the equanimity of their lives. There are those who can't be bothered to get the facts and make up their own minds; they would rather dismiss the whole matter as nonsense, because someone who holds their respect says it is nonsense. There are those who fear for their social security, and will therefore have no part of anything which might place it in jeopardy. There are those who say our science works and gives us many things which we would not otherwise have. What is wrong with that? Why discard it? There are probably as many private reasons for not facing up to the facts as there are people who refuse to do so. However, it is consoling to realize that, through the humble and often criticized comic strip and science fiction stories, the younger generation is being conditioned to accept the reality of people from elsewhere, and when given the opportunity to do so avidly assimilate all they can get on flying saucers and the people who fly them.

The question may well be asked, what of the future? This question has been posed many times, and to the people from outside. The answer: we don't know for sure but we are aware of trends. But considering our limited means for gathering data we must of necessity do a vastly inferior job of predicting events. Our experience has been that when they choose to do so, the people from outside can be quite accurate in their predictions.

We may summarize' the entire flying saucer picture as follows. We have arrived at a time in our development when we must make a final choice between right and wrong. The people from elsewhere are much concerned about the choice which we will make, partly because it will have its repercussions on them and, partly because we are their blood brothers, they are truly concerned with our welfare. There is a cosmic law against interfering in the affairs of others, so they are not allowed to help us directly even though they could easily do so. We must make our own choice of our own free will. Present trends indicate a series of events which may require the help of these people and they stand by ready and willing to render that help. In fact, they have already helped us a great deal, along lines which do not interfere with our freedom of choice. In time, when certain events have transpired, and we are so oriented that we can accept these people from elsewhere, they will meet us freely on the common ground of mutual understanding and trust, and we will be able to learn from them and bring about the Golden Age all men everywhere desire deep within their hearts.

THE BATTLE FOR MAN'S MIND

I propose to give the reader a warning of a grave danger which we are all, consciously or unconsciously, facing in a world in which two great forces are striving to gain control of man's mind. This struggle has been going on from time immemorial, but never in the world's history has the conflict been more intense than it is in this present era of confusion and unrest. In the old days, mankind was often made to suffer physically, unspeakable things in the name of power, but today, with man's mind more developed and better educated, he is now facing the prospect of a refinement of even greater mental and spiritual cruelty – unless he is prepared to protect himself with right thinking.

The two great forces involved in trying to influence man's thinking may be described as positive, i.e., thoughts in harmony with the concept of a love of God and the brotherhood of man, and negative, those encompassing anti-Christ motives designed to gain control over man for the purpose of power. This battle for Man's mind is being waged on two fronts, the physical and the metaphysical, and the object of the fight is to bring about either the spiritual salvation or destruction of homo sapiens.

To deal first with the physical aspects, no matter how hard we may all strive to be strong-minded and individualistic, we are all subtly influenced by the spoken and written word and other forms of thought communication, particularly through the medium of books, newspapers, radio and television.

In the latter field, as the sponsors know only too well, even the "commercials" play an important role in making up our minds to purchase certain products. In our business and social lives, we are often swayed by the thoughts of others and some people, too apathetic to form opinions themselves, are willing to accept the views of others more articulate as their own. In all our daily contacts, a little of the good, bad or indifferent, as the case may be, is rubbing off on us and influencing our thinking.

In the field of politics, often an area of great misrepresentation in order to gain votes, even greater pressures are brought to bear and we are often influenced by the seemingly convincing rhetoric of clever politicians. But it is in the area of international politics that the gravest dangers lie, for here the stakes are high and the lust for power the greatest. Because of this, many of us have been through the horrors of at least one world war, if not two. But let us first analyze how these two wars came about in the first place. In each case, a few men in power, with great personal magnetism, were able to influence and organize the minds of the common people to such a degree of mass-hypnotism that the entire nation believed it had a true cause to fight for. Many of us watched, and history books have recorded, the militarist building-up of Fascism and Nazism and, because of the evil it spawned which the Free World had to fight against, we eventually witnessed the final downfall and disaster brought to these misguided people who allowed their minds to be warped by avaricious despots seeking only greater power. Unity in a country is a fine thing when it is directed into channels for the good of its people, but when it seeks to persecute others in order to gain its ends, it becomes a thing of evil and a triumph for the negative forces.

Crushing the evil forces of World War II, however, did not bring peace to the world and very soon after and for exactly the same reason, i.e., a few men in power masterminding the masses, we found ourselves involved in the long, drawn-out "Cold War" with the U.S.S.R., and hovering on the brink of a third global war which could well end in total annihilation of every living creature on this planet. We can perhaps take some comfort from the fact that the odds against anyone surviving a nuclear war are so great that it is very unlikely that either side will be the first to press the panic button, and maybe it is for this reason that the Russians are turning to a more subtle weapon – the manipulation of man's mind. Their success with the Pavlov experiments and the subsequent "brainwashing" techniques led them a step further – the establishment of an extensive psychical research program, with the main emphasis on mental telepathy and ESP. How far they have gone with this program, we do not know, but one well-known American columnist found it necessary to warn the U.S. government that the newly-developed Russian technique of "cloud busting" (an expression used to describe the production of physical effects by intense mental concentration) would bear their close investigation. The Soviets evidently realize the potentialities of the power of thought far better than we do, and we must remember that power of any kind can be used for either good or evil.

Going to another part of the world, some grave concern is being experienced not only by Japanese intellectuals but outside observers regarding the development of the Soka Gakkai movement in Japan. Soka Gakkai, literally meaning "Value Creation School," is a religious group that developed from Buddhism and became very powerful after the last war. In the early postwar years, it met the needs of a confused people crushed by defeat and horrified at the results of the atom bomb. The Soka Gakkai philosophy expounded, promising the pursuit of happiness and the answering of all problems and setbacks through the medium of constant prayer, made a popular appeal to the masses, and the movement now claims to have several million families as followers. However, as they gained power, the Soka Gakkai leaders, not content with solving domestic problems in the field of religion, became more ambitious and decided not only to try to convert the rest of the world to Soka Gakkai thinking, but also to enter the realm of politics which they considered needed "purifying."

In the area of world conversion, they claim to have many thousands of overseas followers, and they have already set up branches in North America and Southeast Asia, whilst in the field of politics, they have met with considerable success and now hold many seats in local congresses and 15 seats in the Upper House of the Diet. However, with the swelling ranks of the Soka Gakkai becoming more aggressive in their attempts to convert others and more militaristic in their political rallies, the situation is being viewed with considerable alarm, not only by many Japanese but also by the outside world. Anyone who has seen newsreels or television programs showing the disciplined might of the huge Soka Gakkai meetings and rallies, will immediately note that they bear a frightening resemblance to the early Fascist and Nazi demonstrations. Here we have another example of the masterminding of the masses in what appears to be a militant religion whose aims are boldly stated as "The Salvation of Mankind" and "The Spiritual Domination of the World." That the Soka Gakkai realizes the power of thought is made obvious by their slogan "Power Comes From Prayer." The question is: power for what? When a religious group, with several million followers, enters the field of politics, the situation can become fraught with danger, for seldom are religion and politics compatible. One usually has to give way to the other, and unless religious principles for the benefit and not domination of mankind are strictly adhered to, the results could prove disastrous. On the other hand, if the Soka Gakkai movement can succeed in purifying politics and it works earnestly for the happiness and welfare of its followers, then it would indeed prove a wonderful thing, but its present methods of gaining power leave it as a big question mark,

These then are some of the factors we are facing in the battle for Man's mind on the physical plane. But what of the metaphysical influences at work on us – the invisible but all-powerful forces on the purely mental plane?

Whether we realize it or not, we are equally susceptible, if not more so at the subconscious level, to these more subtle influences. Man's brain, which in reality operates on the metaphysical plane, is like a two-way radio which transmits and receives messages along the airwaves of the universe, and his receiving mechanism is open to thoughts both good and bad, which he either accepts or rejects according to his stage of evolution. Most of us are well aware of the truth of mental telepathy and many of us have had personal experiences of thought communication between loved ones often thousands of miles away. But what of special thoughts being beamed at us deliberately for a specific purpose, at both the conscious and subconscious levels, from another plane of existence?

Messages received through esoteric sources, purporting to come from Space Brothers who take an active interest in the spiritual welfare of the inhabitants of our planet, warn us that an even greater conflict is being fought on the metaphysical plane where intelligent beings, of both a higher and a lower spiritual order than ourselves, are waging a fierce battle for Man's mind. The lower or negative forces that damned themselves by wrong thinking are projecting strong thoughts Earthward in an attempt to bring about our spiritual downfall. On the other hand, Space Brothers and other spiritual guardians of our planet are concentrating equally hard on sending out positive thoughts of goodwill and brotherly love. Thus we are being bombarded from the metaphysical plane by two conflicting schools of thought, and, free will being the criterion of spiritual advancement, it is left to us which we choose to accept. However, from a purely logical point of view, if we want to save ourselves a lot of sorrow both in this life and lives to come, we should arm ourselves mentally against the onslaught of negative thoughts.

This is no time for confused or apathetic thinking – often the future breeding-ground of negative thoughts. Nor should we be just receivers and disseminators of the thoughts we pick up. Rather, we should get on the transmitting end and constantly project positive thoughts of goodwill to all.

Every positive thought neutralizes a negative thought, so we shall be serving not only ourselves but all humanity. In the final analysis, there are two simple, clear-cut maxims to be observed for complete protection from the negative forces at work on this planet: (1) Acknowledgment and love of God as the Father of all Creation, and (2) brotherly love extended to all His creatures throughout the universe.

Anything else which interferes with these two beliefs should be vigorously rejected. Further, if we return love for hate, hate will die of malnutrition, for it can only feed on returned hatred. Let us rather pray for spiritual enlightenment for these wretched souls who seek to harm us.

In conclusion, if any of you have doubts about the veracity of the telepathic and inspirational messages received from Space Brothers and others interested in the welfare of our planet, just ask yourselves this one vital question: "Are these messages good and true and for the benefit of mankind on Earth?" If, as you surely must, you come up with an answer of "Yes," then it is obvious that it is the hand of God at work, no matter what medium He chooses to use.

PROJECT MAGNET

MESSAGES TO OTHER WORLDS

The Ottawa Journal of March 23, 1962, carried a story by John W. Finney of Washington. D.C., entitled "Messages To Other Worlds Too Costly, Say Scientists." Partial quotations will develop the theme. "The scientists told the congressmen that life may well have developed on distant planets, but they were gloomy about ever establishing radio contact. They doubted that legislators on other planets, any more than on Earth, would put up the money to build the expensive transmitters needed to send messages to other worlds." These are most significant words and illustrate how deeply we have worn the rut of our thinking! We are so enamored by our own way of thinking and doing things, that we have no place in our consciousness for any other way.

In the first place, there is the basic and quite unjustified assumption that intelligent life on other planets must of necessity follow the pattern which we have set, and have legislators. Also, it is implied that such life would use money as we use it, and put its control in the hands of legislators, and that any program in the broad interests of the race would be determined by them. From what we know of the civilizations "elsewhere," nothing could be farther from the truth!

In the second place, there is the further assumption that any communication between planets must use radio as we know it, within the range of frequencies which we have been able to exploit. Also, that efficient and sufficient transmission means must of necessity be "expensive." There is another point which may not be so readily apparent – and that is the question of language. We communicate, one to another, by means of vocal noises which, by mutual understanding, are coded to carry as nearly as possible the meanings which we desire to convey. But there is no assurance that beings from elsewhere use sound for communicating, and again, from what we have learned from them, their communication means are as far beyond radio as radio is beyond jungle drums.

Quoting further from this news story, ". . . . . transmitters to send signals transit of space is strictly limited to our concept of the velocity of light." What communications we have had with extraterrestrials, in which we have a degree of confidence, have indicated that this is positively not the case, and our concept of the velocity of light is quite erroneous. We have been told, and there is good laboratory evidence to support the statement, that the velocity of light is quite dependent on where and how it is determined and has all sorts of values, and that time itself is far from being fixed, and that there is no such thing as a limiting velocity, except that imposed by the methods used.

The story goes on to quote Dr. Lovell as saying: "To do the job properly will require a number of finely instrumented radio telescopes developed to attack the problem on a long-term basis. There is doubt that any nation would be willing to take on a project so expensive and speculative."

However, nations do spend many times the cost of such a project on research which is not a bit less speculative, and out of which we can hope for only one small step forward. But contact with beings elsewhere in the universe, if they are appreciably more advanced than we are, could yield knowledge which would take us forward, not by steps, but by leaps and bounds! Or, for a change, we could send out details of our science for the benefit of races not quite so developed as we are – broadcast our culture and propaganda to the universe at large, to let them know what we have that we are proud of!

PROJECT MAGNET

PROJECT MAGNET—THE CANADIAN UFO STUDY

Project Magnet was authorized in December 1950, following my request to the Canadian Department of Transport for permission to make use of the Department's laboratory and field facilities in a study of unidentified flying objects and physical principles which might appear to be involved.

The program consisted of two parts. The first part was the collecting of as much high quality data as possible, analyzing it, and where possible drawing conclusions from it. The second part consisted of a systematic questioning of all our basic concepts in the hopes of turning up a discrepancy which might prove to be the key to a new technology.

Unfortunately, the program was plagued by well-meaning but misguided journalists who were looking for spectacular copy which could be turned to a political account, to such an extent that both those who were working on the project and the Department of Transport found themselves in an embarrassed position. Consequently, when the Project Magnet report was made and permission sought to extend the scope of the investigation through federal financial support, the decision was finally made in 1954 that this would not be advisable in the face of the publicity from which the whole project had suffered.

Project Magnet was officially dropped by the Department of Transport in 1954, although the Department indicated its willingness to permit the continued use of laboratory facilities, provided that this could be done at no cost to the public treasury. The project continued under these conditions, and to this extent may be said to have gone underground. The government of Canada was therefore not participant in the continuation of the project and not in any way responsible for its conclusions.

The conclusions reached by Project Magnet and contained in its official report were based on a rigid statistical analysis of sighting reports and were as follows:

1. There is a 91% probability that at least some of the sightings were of real objects of unknown origin.

2. There is about a 60% probability that these objects are alien vehicles.

PROJECT MAGNET

The conclusions based on studies of the basic physical concepts were as follows:

1. Many of our fundamental concepts are inherently ambiguous and quite a different philosophy can be built up on the alternatives.

2. Several of these alternatives lead to much simpler arithmetic, and presentations which do not have to resort to patchwork corrections to make them all embracing.

3. Furthermore, some of our ideas with respect to fields and their behavior are wrong.

Project Magnet activities dealt with following up any and all leads. Many of these leads were dead ends, but a few were quite significant and well worth the overall effort. At the present time a definite pattern is emerging, and the ground work is being laid for a new technology which may literally lead us to the stars.

THE DAY PROJECT MAGNET DETECTED A FLYING SAUCER

August 8, 1954, began as a rather typical day at Project Magnet. Since the project had started it was hoped that the instruments on hand would sooner or later pick up an unidentified flying object and track and analyze its movements. For months I and my tiny group of like-minded associates had watched the sensitive gravimeter in vain. On occasions when large commercial airliners would pass over, our hearts would skip a beat as the instruments would register aerial activities.

But on August 8 at 3:01 P.M., the gravimeter began acting strangely. First it wavered slightly, drawing a thin dark line on the graph paper being used to register the movements of the instruments. Without further warning the gravimeter went wild. All evidence indicated that a real unidentified flying object had flown within feet of the station. Alarm systems connected to the instrument panel began to ring, alerting us to the UFO. After watching the instruments a few seconds, we ran outside to see what was causing the odd reaction. Unfortunately our area was completely fogged in, and whatever was up there could not be seen visually.

(Editor's note: Later, while making a public statement, it was reported that Smith was very careful in stating that the object "might" have been a flying saucer, discounting the possibility that it could have been any sort of airplane. Several years later, while being interviewed on national Canadian TV, Smith commented that flying saucers were responsible for a number of "things" then happening in Canadian skies. He, however, did not take the time to explain further. No official release has ever been made by the Department of Transport, or any other Canadian government authority, on the "flying saucer" that was tracked over Project Magnet on Aug. 8, 1954.-T.G.B.)

PROJECT MAGNET

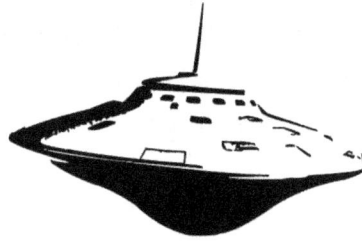

THE FIVE FACES OF MAN

When we enter this physical universe, we find that there are five relationships to which we are subject. An understanding of these relationships is necessary for a successful sojourn here and progress to higher planes. Not only do the majority of us remain in ignorance of these relationships, but many of us do not even recognize their existence. It is true that there are certain ones which are of interest to us and we do a little lip service there for purely selfish reasons, but there is almost no recognition of the essential nature of these five relationships.

The first relationship is religion, which is the relationship of a being to its creator. Here we have a hodgepodge of superstition dressed up in pageantry giving lip service to something in which few people actually believe, and practically no one knows anything about. Every great religion says "Love thy God!" but how many understand what this means? We think we know family love, love of country, love of things, but do we know love of God?

Love thy God as thyself. This is something a bit nearer to our understanding because we are all pretty selfish creatures; but again do we really know what it means? Do those of us who abuse our bodies and minds with the many and varied current malpractices have any understanding of what it means to love ourselves?

Love thy God with all thy heart, with all thy soul and with all thy mind.

Here again we are urged to a definite course of action which is spelled out rather clearly, and again we do little or nothing about it. We must learn to know our hearts, our souls, and our minds: to know their capacity and then to use this capacity. There is a tremendous potential here if we but understand it.

The hierarchy is the relationship of a being to others not of its kind. In this universe we know very little about the hierarchy beyond the few other living things which share this planet with us, and which we regard with disdain as being of little or no consequence. We have little knowledge of the vast realms of beings of higher evolution than ourselves and when we do experience a little impact from them, we ignore and suppress it and hope that it will go away because it embarrasses us. There are very few people on Earth who do not feel that somehow they are the acme of Creation and there are none greater, except possibly a vague and nebu-

64

lous deity with which we have little or nothing in common. And yet, knowledge of the hierarchy obviously is necessary if we are to progress in it; for we are a part of it whether we realize it or not.

Civilization is the relationship of beings with others of the same kind. This is something about which we know a little, but don't do very much. We have a civilization of sorts but it isn't very good, not nearly so good as the civilizations developed by the ants and the bees. We have a general idea of what a civilization ought to be and we all have dreams of a utopia, but we have not yet mastered even the basic principles upon which a successful civilization must be based.

The many ideologies and 'isms are all attempts to develop a more satisfactory civilization and each must be regarded as a stepping stone leading toward the ultimate. As long as there is disagreement about how civilization should be set up, just that long will it continue to evolve. When people on this planet are satisfied with their civilization it will crystallize as has the civilization of the ants and the bees, and further evolvement will rest entirely with the individuals. Because of the basic restless nature of our branch of mankind we will probably not settle for a civilization pattern in the near future, and our ultimate civilization will bear little resemblance to what we have now. But the important thing is to recognize that what we have isn't very good and the ultimate is still far off, and we should work toward it.

Science is the relationship of a being to the physical world in which it exists. We have evolved a science of sorts by observing Nature and guessing at the causes of the phenomena which we observe. When we have guessed a plausible explanation we test it by asking Nature a few experimental questions and then fitting the answers into our hypothesis. If they can be made to fit we assume that our original guess was right and we then proceed gleefully on to the next guess. By following this method we have built up a most magnificent concept of this universe in which we live, all beautifully supported by mathematical analyses, and almost entirely self-consistent.

Although it is not generally admitted in scientific circles, there is a prime Cause for this universe, called the Creator, and this universe was established from and within Nothing-At-All. What we observe is the end product of this creation, or at least that stage of it which involves us. What we do not see is the mechanism by which this all came about and, so long as we insist on inspecting it from our rather limited point of view, we are not likely to find out very much about its inherent structure. However, if we follow the path trodden by the Creator and start as He did, from Nothing-At-All and follow up the logical sequences, from the bottom up, checking with Nature by experiment every so often we can get quite a different view of this universe which is ever so much simpler and probably much more accurate than that of our conventional science. By definition science is the relationship of a being with the physical world in which it exists, so it is fairly obvious that the viewpoint should be that of the being, i.e., an emanation of the Creator following the path set by the Creator.

The relationship of the being to the physical vehicle which it occupies is the Tallus, and this is an area where understanding is most conspicuous by its absence. Unfortunately, many, many people do not even recognize that there is such a relationship, believing that the physical vehicle is the being, in spite of the vast amount of evidence which is apparent to all that the being is quite apart, though intimately associated with the physical vehicle. The subtraction of limbs or organs does not detract from a being and the retirement of a being from its physical vehicle is not necessarily related too closely with such subtractions. The transcendental nature of awareness and impossibility of localizing it within a physical structure indicates that it is something separate.

We are accustomed to living in our physical bodies and to us it feels "normal" and any deviation from this condition results in feelings and sensations which are unique. If our thresholds are depressed as in sleep or under anesthetic we can alter the relationships of our beings to our vehicles without undue disturbance, but on the other hand, if our thresholds are raised any such alteration becomes most apparent. These are the Tallic sensations or experiences, and are an essential part of our experience here.

Drugs, excitement and many other stimuli simultaneously raise our thresholds and allow alteration of the Tallus relationship. The group of experiences involving sex, birth, death and mediumship all involve closely related physical sensations caused by the partial (or complete) withdrawal of the being from the physical vehicle, or some rearrangement in relation thereto.

These then, are the five relationships which make up the experience of a being in a physical environment. They are part and parcel of our lives and their understanding is an essential part of our evolvement. We have but a scanty appreciation of these relationships, and even to many they do not exist except as philosophies or superstitions. However, we have only to look at what little is apparent of our brothers from elsewhere to appreciate the results of better understanding of these basic relationships; and they tell us that they too, have a long way to go!

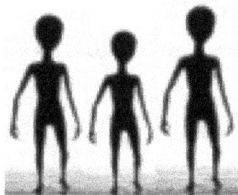

BINDING FORCES

Matter, as we know it, is held together by "forces" the nature of which we do not clearly understand. We have developed some very elegant theories to explain most of the observed phenomena, and we add sufficient "correction factors" to make the theory fit the rest. But every now and then we come face to face with something which our theory just will not explain, and rather than admit that our theory is inadequate, discard it and start over again, we just can't bring ourselves to throw out such an elegant mathematical masterpiece, so we usually just turn our backs on the new fact and refuse to recognize it. This is well demonstrated in the matter of binding forces.

Some years ago, following some rather bad aeroplane crashes for which there was no satisfactory explanation, the people from "elsewhere" were asked through "contacts" if these crashes were possibly due to our craft flying too close to their craft. We were informed that while a very few of our craft had suffered in this manner much greater care was now being exercised by the saucer pilots so that this cause was virtually eliminated. We were informed, however, that our pilots flew around in complete disregard of the regions of reduced binding with which this planet is afflicted, and very often their craft were not designed with a sufficient factor of safety and came apart.

A COUNTER ARGUMENT

When we countered by saying that we knew nothing of such regions, we were informed that means for detecting them were easily within our technology and that we should build suitable instruments and then pay attention to what they registered. They also passed a few uncomplimentary remarks about our propensity for shooting off atom bombs which actually created a pair of such "vortices" with each explosion.

The principle of the "Binding Meter" was then explained to us, and we were left to work out its detailed design. The principle is quite simple: all matter is held together by the relative configurations of the three basic fields of nature, tempic, electric and magnetic. These configurations are characteristic of what we call the molecular structure, and the interactions of these fields is linear. Therefore, since the fields interacting are the sums of the local fields, and the background fields, such interaction can be used to indicate certain characteristics of the background, through this very nonlinearity.

Structurally, the binding meter consists of a nylon fiber which is stressed close to its elastic limit (after having been overstressed to establish stability) pulling against a steel spring which is stressed well below its elastic limit. The nylon fiber is wound around a spindle which carries a pointer so that any longitudinal movement of the fiber will cause the spindle to turn and the pointer to move across an arbitrary scale. In setting up the instrument nylon fishing leader was used and pre-stressed to the breaking point and this point noted. The instrument was then threaded and one end fastened to the spring and the other placed under tension to 75 per cent of the previously noted breaking stress, and the end clamped under a friction washer which was somewhat softer than the nylon to grip it solidly without deforming the nylon. The whole instrument was then set aside for a few days to make sure that it was stable, after which the pointer was slipped to mid-scale and the instrument was considered ready for service.

MANY SUCCESSFUL INSTRUMENTS

By making the body of the instrument of aluminum tubing about 1/2 inch diameter and 10 inches long, the combination gives very good temperature compensation, and a range of temperature of 100 F. makes less than % division on an arbitrary scale of 12. There is no perceptible change over the complete range of humidity and no barometric sensitivity was observed.

Dimensions apparently are not critical, and successful instruments have been made with quite a variety of parameters. Unfortunately, we have no way of calibrating these instruments at the present time, and the best we can do is use them for qualitative indication.

My colleagues and I have investigated the general areas through which aircraft have flown just prior to unexplained crashes and we have found several regions of reduced binding, the meters showing several scale divisions change. These regions seem to be roughly circular and about 1,000 ft. in diameter, and probably extend upward quite a distance. A few have been detected by air when planes have flown through them, but fortunately in these cases the craft were strong enough to remain intact.

Whether this is generally true or not we cannot say, but it does appear that things are somewhat stronger in the northern latitudes than they are farther south, and certain areas seem to be permanently afflicted with reduced binding. We do not know if the regions of reduced binding move about or just fade away, but we do know that when we looked for several of them after three or four months we could find no trace of them.

It would therefore appear that this business of reduced binding would stand quite a bit of further serious investigation. Unfortunately, because of the unorthodox source of this information, efforts so far to obtain official recognition have resulted only in more letters being added to the "crank file."

THE COSMIC POLICE FORCE

It has been stated that according to messages purporting to come from the space brothers, our space friends had claimed that if there was a great outpouring of prayer and positive thought issuing from the inhabitants of our world, thus raising the spiritual vibrations of our planet, they could draw on this power to assist us even further. A question put to the space brothers as to exactly what was meant by this statement brought forth an extremely interesting reply which may shed some new light on a vital reason for their presence around planet earth.

The explanation given was that a large number of the space brothers, whose special mission it is to safeguard the spiritual welfare and evolutional progress of earthlings, had banded themselves together to form what might be described in earth terms as a "cosmic police force." The true role of any police force, they added, is a purely defensive one – a protective measure designed to ensure the safety and well-being of society-at-large and the maintenance of law and order to safeguard this objective. This, in effect, is the role that the special contingent of the cosmic police force, dedicated to the protection of inhabitants of earth and the planet itself, is carrying out.

This role is mainly a dual one: (1) to keep at bay negative forces from outer space who attempt to inflict their stronger evil influence on negative and border-line-negative earthlings; and (2) to assure that all outer space beings permitted to visit our world observe strictly the cosmic laws governing noninterference with and non-hostility toward the inhabitants of planet earth. The space brothers emphasize that "(1)" must not be interpreted by war-conscious earthlings as in any way a battle or an act of aggression against negative beings who, they remind us, are still God's creatures but in the early kindergarten stage of spiritual development – quite the reverse, for their method of dealing with such beings is to beam out to them intense thoughts for good will which emanate in the form of a radiant light through which no ungodly thought can penetrate.

The negative forces, being the powers of darkness, are rendered impotent by this strong, pure light of good will and spirituality and, blinded by its dazzling glow, they are unable to carry out their evil intentions. This, say the space brothers, is the only way to deal successfully with negative forces and that we, too, should use this same method. It is fatal to hate or fear them for in so doing we only fall into a trap and lower our own spiritual vibrations. Rather, we should extend good will and have compassion for these backward children of darkness by praying for them, as this way we not only protect ourselves but, good begetting good, we help both them and ourselves.

In the case of "(2)" the space brothers speak of what might be termed as a "United Planets organization," members of which are drawn from planets that have reached a certain level of spiritual enlightenment, but just as it is with our own United Nations organization, some members are more backward than others and a constant vigil must be kept to ensure that they observe fully the cosmic laws laid down in the space charter of this interplanetary organization.

From the foregoing, it will be seen that the main purpose of the protective role of the cosmic police force is to allow the inhabitants of planet earth to evolve on their own merits without any undue influence from either the positive or negative forces. This is cosmic law. Therefore, we must not allow our knowledge of the work of the cosmic police force to lull us into any false sense of security. We are strictly on our own when it comes to spiritual unfoldment for, as the space brothers are quick to point out, while the cosmic police force can protect us from outside influences, it cannot protect us from ourselves or our own free thinking. However, if we, of our own free will, send out sincere prayers and positive thoughts for good, our space friends claim they can use this light force to help us further. It was added that there is an urgent and specific need for this at the moment. Querying this, an interesting factor came to light.

It was explained that the explosion of nuclear devices (a negative force) has not only torn parts of earth's protective atmosphere (which, if continued, may have drastic physical consequences to Man on Earth, involving violent weather patterns, floods, earthquakes and deformed biological mutations caused by increased radioactivity, etc.), but these massive explosions have, by their negative nature, also damaged the metaphysical protective "envelope" surrounding this planet, thus allowing negative astral entities to penetrate through these ripped portions and further influence negative thinking on Earth – hence much of the trouble and strife we are experiencing in our world today. While the cosmic police force can shield us from unwarranted outside negative influences, they cannot protect us from the consequences of negative emanations coming directly from our own planet. This would be contrary to the universal law of karma.

Only we can repair the damage we have created ourselves. This, say our space friends, we can do by sincere prayer for the cessation of nuclear explosions and positive thought envisioning the closing of the gaps in our protective atmosphere and its metaphysical counterpart. Such a spiritual emanation from

71

PROJECT MAGNET

Earth would take the outward form of radiant light with which the space brothers claim that, with our expressed desire to do so, they could mend the torn portions of our atmosphere and thus block further entry of negatives forces. They call on us urgently to play our part in an all-out effort to save ourselves and our planet from the total destruction it is otherwise headed for. Time is running short and we must act now.

ARE WE ENTERING OR LEAVING?

With atomic energy we are crossing a threshold, but are we entering or just leaving? Much has been said and written about the awful devastation which would be caused by an atomic war. It has been suggested – and with just cause – that such a war would probably wipe out civilization, leaving the remnants of the human race in atavistic savagery, if there were any remnants.

Dr. Hugh Keenleyside, former Under Secretary of State for External Affairs for Canada, estimates that there are in existence at the present time more than 150,000 nuclear devices, many more than required to do the job!

Consider what happens when an atom bomb explodes. The fission process which comprises the explosion releases enormous quantities of energy similar to that originating within even the hottest star. If only 10% of the energy available in Uranium 235 of Plutonium were suddenly converted into heat, the temperature of the mass would jump to the order of fifty billion degrees centigrade. Even if the blast were diluted by five hundred times as much inert material as there was active material, the temperature would still be of the order of one hundred million degrees.

Now, the temperature of the sun, as we determine it, is about six thousand degrees on the surface and about ten or twenty million degrees in the interior. It is presumed to derive its energy from the conversion of hydrogen to helium through an intermediate cycle involving carbon, oxygen and nitrogen, which cycle progresses very smoothly at the sun's temperature.

If, however, the sun's temperature were much higher, the hydrogen could convert directly, first into deuterium, tritium, and helium, without benefit of the time delay and stabilizing action of the carbon-nitrogen-oxygen cycle, and would produce most probably an explosion of increasing magnitude which would continue until it either ran out of hydrogen or the eventual expansion of the gases produced a sufficient drop in temperature to stop the reaction.

Suppose that an atom bomb (either fission or fusion type) landed in a large body of fresh water such as one of our Great Lakes, and furthermore, that it sank to a considerable depth before exploding. The explosion, when it did take place would be confined by walls of water consisting largely of hydrogen, since two thirds of the atoms in water are hydrogen. Before the bubble of hot gases resulting from the explosion could overcome the inertia of the water and rise to the surface, it is almost certain that the water directly in contact with the blast would be heated to temperatures comparable with that of the blast, itself, one hundred million degrees or hotter. At such temperature the hydrogen in the water would be in prime condition to convert directly into helium and would in fact become a "hydrogen bomb" with the release of about the same or greater energy per unit mass as was released from the active material of the bomb itself.

Consequently, a thermonuclear chain reaction would probably set in which would be cumulative and self-propagating. Once initiated it would continue increasing in intensity until stopped by either a lack of hydrogen or the eventual drop in temperature of the expanding gases. In any case the reaction would probably persist until most of the available hydrogen had gone up in helium.

Should such a thing happen even by accident, and an atom bomb explode deep in one of our fresh water lakes, with thousands of tons of hydrogen available, there could result a blast of such intensity that it would envelop the entire planet in a few seconds, vaporizing everything on its surface and maybe even shattering the core, and producing a celestial display visible throughout our galaxy. Unfortunately we would be in no position to observe it as we would have ceased to exist.

The foregoing is not idle speculation. It is based on the same data, calculations and measurements which produced the atom bomb, and the fact of the bomb is grim testimony to its potentialities. We may well ask ourselves the question: we are crossing the threshold, but are we entering or just leaving?

PROJECT MAGNET

THE MYSTERIOUS CHUNK OF HARDWARE

On the outside property of the headquarters of the Ottawa New Sciences Club there lies a large piece of metal – an unidentified object which has so far baffled all attempts at positive identification and over which an aura of mystery hangs as to its exact composition, purpose, origin and most of all, the unusual circumstances surrounding the finding of this large chunk of hardware in the St. Lawrence river of Quebec. This piece of metal measures about 4 ft. by 6 ft. and is roughly oval in shape, somewhat like an inverted mushroom, i.e., flat on top and roughly hemispherical on the underside. A plug or post about 9" in diameter, at 90 degrees to the flat surface, penetrates the center of the mass and extends through top and bottom surfaces. A smaller protuberance, which may be the remains of a ZW' pipe, appears out of the flat surface near the plug. The weight is estimated at about 3,000 pounds. The whole is made up of layers of material which evidently have been subjected to very high temperatures and pressure.

The material is ferrous, extremely hard, and resistant to all attempts to cut or dismantle it. It is faintly magnetic until melted, when it seems to acquire approximately the magnetic permeability of mild steel. Because articles on this mystery metal have recently appeared in newspapers containing a number of inaccuracies with regard to the facts of the case as we know them in Ottawa, we propose to give our readers a brief account of the history of the metal as far as we know it.

According to an early account which appeared in a French language newspaper in Quebec on June 12, 1960, between 3:00 and 4:00 A. M., EDT, a sonic boom rocked the area around Quebec City. At about the same time, a fiery object fell out of the sky, splitting at about one to two thousand feet altitude, into two pieces, one somewhat larger than the other. Both fell into the St. Lawrence River, near Les Ecureils, about 20 miles upriver from Quebec City. The smaller piece was quite close to the shore and visible at low tide; the other lay close to the shipping lane and was completely submerged.

It should, however, be pointed out that when, shortly afterward, a group of club members carried out an investigation at the actual location, they were un-

75

able to find anyone in the Les Ecureils area who had actually heard or seen the metal fall – strange, in such a small town. So the manner in which the metal arrived at the scene still remains a mystery.

THE AREA

At Les Ecureils, the river bank drops sharply to a relatively flat shale bed which extends for nearly a quarter of a mile to the deep water shipping channel. The channel is separated from the shale area by a jumble of large boulders. The river is tidal so that the area of the find varies from dry to a maximum depth of water of about 1½ feet.

THE FIND

A local resident, who supplements his income by beachcombing, covered the area pretty thoroughly the first day or two of June. Then came three days of rain during which he did not work the area. When the weather cleared, he found the two pieces of metal on the shale bed.

DEPOSITION OF THE METAL

The finder, unable to handle the larger chunk, loaded the small 800-lb. piece and sold it for one cent a pound to a scrap metal dealer in Quebec City where it was erroneously classified as nonferrous metal. The large magnetic crane, used for handling the scrap, would not lift the metal due to its low magnetic permeability, so it was pushed into a pile of nonferrous scrap and eventually shipped to Japan. As for the larger piece of metal, rumor of the find reached the Canadian Arsenals Research and Development Establishment (CARDE) in the area, which, thinking it might have been part of a space capsule, picked it up for investigation. On completion of their investigations, CARDE eventually handed the metal over to a club member who, at great difficulty, trailered the heavy object to Ottawa where it is now in the custody of the club.

THE FINDINGS

After analysis, CARDE reached the following conclusions:

Top: The mysterious chunk of metal as photographed in a Canadian government laboratory where it underwent a limited amount of tests and analyses by the late Wilbert B. Smith. The white lines shown on the metal were placed there by WBS for identification purposes.

Bottom: Shows one of the inclusions on the outer surface of the metal taken with the aid of microphotography.

"The X-ray diffraction analysis indicated that the unidentified object consisted of a metallic face-centered cubic compound, with a unit-cell dimension agreeing with those of (1) austenitic steel, and (2) meteoric iron.

PROJECT MAGNET

"The semi-quantitative spectrographic analysis showed, however, that there was insufficient nickel present for the material to be of meteoric origin. The amount of manganese detected in the spectrographic analysis suggests that the metallic material is best described as high-manganese austenitic steel. This is consistent with the very weak ferromagnetic nature of the metal. The iron oxide and the hydrated iron oxides on the surface are normal results of the exposure of steel to the atmosphere. The amounts of quartz and calcite detected by X-ray diffraction are very small, and are common extraneous materials. The low nickel and high manganese content are not consistent with a meteoric origin, whereas they are consistent with common high-tensile steels. The object is therefore considered to be of terrestrial origin."

Another report states in part: "The metal object proved to be a mass of high strength metal which had fallen, or had been dropped, while in a plastic state, and had splattered like a ball of mud. It was 6 ft. in diameter and 2 ft. thick at the center. At the center of the body, there was an outline of a tube about 10 inches in diameter which protruded from the mass about 6 inches.

"A small electronic potting can was imbedded near one of the outer edges. By scratching away the potting plastic, it was possible to identify an electronic component which appeared to be a transistor. There was also the imprint of another electronic can which appeared to have been removed by curio seekers. It is not considered that the object fell in the location where it was found, because there was no crater or splattered material in the vicinity. The tidal flats at this point are solid rock. An analysis by CARDE revealed that the metal is an alloy with high manganese content. CARDE personnel who are familiar with foundry operations, consider it to be a normal product of a foundry consisting of slag with semi-molten scrap imbedded. Their investigation did not reveal any electronic components."

Despite the findings of CARDE, an element of doubt exists as to whether these are completely accurate. Although they considered the object to be of terrestrial origin, laboratory experiments on the metal carried out by the late Wilbert B. Smith and coworkers, resulted in a number of unusual reactions not consistent with the normal behavior of terrestrial metal. This was most evident when a small piece of the metal was heated with an acetylene torch which caused it to blossom into a miniature white cloud with extremely bright sparks in it – a sort of A-bomb in miniature. WBS concluded that the magnesium went exothermic, reduced the ferrite in the spinnel crystal structure, formed the cloud and left the iron free to burn with O_2 in the air.

He warned that anyone attempting to heat a larger chunk of the metal might very well fry himself! He also considered that the intense heating should have burned the object worse than it did and he therefore reached the conclusion that it could not have been a blast furnace product. Further experiments revealed that some parts of the metal could not stand too much heat, thus limiting the possibilities as to why such a manufactured item came to grief. In testing the metal with the acetylene torch, it was noted that the resulting sphere, with its intensely brilliant shower of sparks, burned until nothing remained – with no residue or slag common with Earth metals.

CARDE suggested that the metal may have been slag from a foundry brought to the area via an ice floe. The facts of the case, however, do not bear this out. The nearest mills are many miles from Ecureils – and it was the month of June! The material is not a common foundry product, and even if it had been, one wonders why the foundry would waste 3,000 pounds of metal!

MORE MYSTERIES

How the metal arrived at Les Ecureils remains the biggest mystery of all. The maximum depth of water at high tide and the closely-spaced boulders along the shipping channel would seem to rule out any possibility of arrival by boat or raft. Had it fallen from the sky, the noise would have been earth-shaking. Even a small meteorite sounds like a rushing freight train.

A further mystery, indicating the possibility of exposure of the metal in outer space, is that the outer surface, under powerful magnification, shows minute inclusions which well may be micrometeorites picked up during a long sojourn in space. The Club has in its possession a series of photographs of the outer surface of the metal, taken with the aid of microphotography, in which these inclusions can be observed quite clearly. The density of these particles is about 30 per square centimeter. Dr. Peter Millman of the Canada National Research Council, estimated that micrometeorites of this size would occur through a sq. cm. section at about $10-6$, so it would take about a year to accumulate such a density.

Analyses. Several chemical analyses of the metal have been made by the club. These vary, indicating that the mass is not homogeneous. To date, the club has been unable to find any organization with the proper facilities willing to carry out a mass spectrographic analysis to determine the number of isotopes in the various elements contained in the metal. If this could be done, it would establish whether or not the material is of terrestrial origin, although, of course, there is always the possibility that other planets may have the same minerals as Earth. And even if it were proved to be of terrestrial origin, there still remains the intriguing mystery of how it arrived on the beach!

[EDITOR'S NOTE: Since the original article on the "Mysterious Chunk" was written, additional information has been gathered and new evidence formulated which suggests that this "finding" may well represent evidence of some sort of unearthly material.]

PROJECT MAGNET

UNIDENTIFIED HARDWARE MYSTERY DEEPENS

As a result of a plea for UFO hardware for laboratory tests as put forward by Dr. J. Allen Hynek in his article, "White Paper on UFOs" (Christian Science Monitor, May 23, 1967), the Ottawa New Sciences Club had written to Dr. Edward Condon, heading the group of University of Colorado scientists commissioned by the USAF to investigate the UFO problem, enclosing a copy of the foregoing and suggesting that his group might consider it worthy of further analysis in view of the somewhat mysterious circumstances surrounding the finding of the metal and subsequent tests on it. This letter was sent on June 21, 1967, and during the 3-month period of silence that followed, it was ascertained that a good many others who had written to Colorado had received the same "silence" treatment – not even an acknowledgment of their letters. On Sept. 11, 1967, our club secretary wrote again to Dr. Condon, this time by registered mail, requesting a reply to the offer made by the club. On Sept. 22, 1967, a reply was received from Dr. Condon's secretary, apologizing for the delay and stating that the matter had now been placed in the hands of a Dr. Roy Craig.

On Sept. 29, a letter was received from Dr. Craig, the first paragraph of which reads: "Your letter to Dr. Condon written on June 21, 1967, recently came to my attention. The piece of metallic material you mentioned, since it cannot be related directly to an unidentified flying object, would not seem of sufficient value to our study to warrant further analysis by us."

This cursory brush-off was not entirely unexpected, as by this time we had gained the distinct impression, from colleagues in the U.S. and elsewhere, that the Colorado project was not an all-out effort to solve the UFO mystery and was likely to be overshadowed by USAF policy.

What followed in Dr. Craig's letter, however, was decidedly intriguing, as it consisted of a request to supply him with copies of official reports from the Canadian "Project Magnet," as he had failed to obtain them from another "source." One can only wonder at the manner in which the Colorado project was being conducted, as surely the obvious thing would have been to request this material from the Canadian government department concerned – or could it be that the Canadian government was not "playing ball" in this regard? This, in turn, would seem to raise the question of exactly how much cooperation exists between Canada and the U.S.A. in their respective governmental UFO research programs.

In view of recent developments in connection with the chunk of hardware at Ottawa (more of which to follow) we cannot help but think that Dr. Condon, in turning down our offer, may have missed a wonderful opportunity to produce something concrete in his UFO findings – unless, of course, something positive is not exactly what he was looking for. Dr. Condon's public statements on UFO matters have not reflected a particularly positive attitude.

PROJECT MAGNET

To quote an extract from the NICAP publication "The UFO Investigator" of Oct. 1967: "Several times, however, Dr. Condon has made negative public statements about UFOs, even though he has taken no part in any field investigations of sightings. Some press media and members of the public have, therefore, questioned Condon's objectivity." With this in mind, plus the "silence" treatment meted out by Colorado to many who have offered constructive suggestions for the solution of the UFO mystery, it is small wonder that many Ufologists and a large proportion of the general public fear a "whitewash" as the outcome of the investigation. Further doubts are added to general misgivings by a careful study of the AF-Colorado contract as published in the Nov/Dec, 1967 issue of "UFO Investigator".

While NICAP officials who have worked with the Colorado project scientists at Boulder are convinced of the individual integrity of most of these men and reject the idea that all of them would enter into any secret deal with the AF, nevertheless they do point up some strange inclusions in the contract which arouse suspicions that the USAF expected a negative finding. These strange items refer to Sections B1 and B2 and deal with a speeding up of the publicity plan and in particular, the project scientists' public statements.

NICAP queries why the AF should be so anxious to speed up these statements and goes on to say: "Some critics who have been dubious from the start about an AF-financed project, may now be convinced they were right. In writing Sections B1 and B2 into the contract, they may say the AF must even then have been fairly sure of a negative conclusion-in short, a 'whitewash.'" They also suggest another possibility: that at the time the contract was drawn up, "relatively few influential scientists had publicly rejected the AF answers, though many have since done so. The AF representatives might have felt certain no group of reputable scientists would accept UFO reality. It may have seemed a safe gamble to prepare this extraordinary program to put over a negative answer." However, NICAP points out that the Colorado scientists were not bound to follow the AF plan, although the contract strongly urged them to cooperate. Apparently, already there is disagreement among the scientists, and herein lies our only hope, plus NICAP's promise to do all in its power to further an impartial scientific investigation. We should all be extremely grateful for NICAP's untiring efforts in this direction.

A word of praise should also be recorded for the Colorado scientists themselves, especially those who have worked objectively on a number of diverse UFO studies. One of these includes the compilation of a worldwide bibliography of UFO literature, and in this regard, the editor of Topside has been approached by the U.S. Library of Congress, which has undertaken to prepare this bibliography for Colorado, asking for cooperation in supplying them with all available writings of the late Wilbert B. Smith, and a complete file of all the issues of Topside, which will be microfilmed. They also asked for recommendations of other UFO publications they should endeavor to acquire. We have been more than happy to cooperate fully on what appears to be a constructive and worthwhile project which, along with other UFO studies, is all to the credit side of the Colorado investigation. It is interesting to recall here that in the Spring, 1965, issue of Topside, the space brothers predicted that governments would be turning to private UFO groups for information!

Meanwhile, what of the situation in Canada? Back in the summer months, we felt encouraged that at long last there was a prospect of something concrete being done to solve the UFO mystery at governmental levels, both in Canada and the U.S.A. Disquieting rumors about the Colorado project had not yet reached us. Our Minister of Defense, the Hon. Paul Hellyer, had released more UFO information to the public, had announced that the National Research Council was planning to set up a special committee to study the UFO problem under the Chairmanship of Dr. R. S. Rettie, Head of Space Research & Facilities Branch of NRC in Ottawa, and had declared himself "open-minded" about UFOs (progress indeed!). Furthermore, in September, Dr. G. N. Patterson, Director of the University of Toronto's Institute for Aerospace Studies, announced that a group of scientists was commencing its own Colorado-type UFO investigation, with the hope of Canadian and U.S. government participation.

Everything looked very hopeful for the future. But then, bit by bit, things began to fall apart at the seams and the whole issue became clouded with doubts, as an apparent change in governmental UFO policy emerged on both sides of the border. In the U.S., doubts were expressed about the genuineness of the Colorado project and there was some sinister talk of the pressuring and silencing of certain private UFO researchers. In Canada, the Hon. Paul Hellyer, to whom Canadian Ufologists had looked with renewed hope and respect, was suddenly transferred from the Department of National Defense to become Minister of Transport. Coming so shortly after his UFO revelations, we could only wonder if there was any link. If so, it is regrettable, from our point of view. His successor, as Minister of National Defense, the Hon. Leo Cadieux, had already made it clear that he was not going to be quite so communicative about UFO matters. On Nov. 6, 1967, in reply to a question raised in the House of Commons as to whether a report arising out of a federal investigation into the case of Stephen Michalek who claimed to have been burned by a landed UFO at Falcon Lake, Manitoba, would be made public, Mr. Cadieux had this to say: "It is not the intent of the Department of National Defense to make public the report of the alleged sighting." This, freely translated, probably means that the "alleged" sighting was genuine!

Meanwhile, Dr. R. S. Rettie was making it evident that his role, as Chairman of the proposed NRC research study on UFOs, was a somewhat reluctant one. In an article which appeared in the Nov., 1967, issue of "Maclean's Magazine," entitled "Look! There's a Flying Saucer!" the author, Jon Ruddy, states that Dr. Rettie "may be Canada's most articulate skeptic on UFOs." There is nothing wrong in a healthy skepticism – most of us started off this way – but it takes a particular brand of courage to admit that one has been wrong in public statements. However, we feel that the blunt and outspoken Dr. Rettie may well be possessed of this type of moral courage – if government policy permits it. We must admit that some of Dr. Rettie's remarks, as quoted in this article, would appear to have a somewhat negative approach. While he is prepared to accept that there are societies elsewhere in the universe well-advanced technologically, he says that he does not believe that they would behave so illogically as to "fool around in flying saucers and approach people in the woods with friendly offers of help."

Physical contact reports he writes off, as "such activities can, I am sure, be dismissed as a prank, as charlatanism, as sensation seeking or, unfortunately, as temporary or permanent mental unbalance." Strong words and a sweeping statement from a scientist who has not yet fully investigated the UFO phenomena. On Jan. 3, 1968, Dr. Rettie stated in an interview that arrangements were nearly complete for the transfer of the responsibility for checking UFO sightings to his branch which, he said, "would 'filter' reports of sightings. Some would be of definite scientific interest, such as reports of meteorites or fireballs." (No mention of UFOs being of scientific interest – strange.) His final comment was: "Part of the role will be in reassuring the public."

Dr. Rettie is right that the public needs reassuring, but not on the reality of UFOs. Five million Americans and probably an equal per capita percentage of Canadians are already convinced that they exist and this belief has caused no panic. More than twenty years of non-hostility from UFOs and the Canadian government's own assurance that they represent no threat to national security have already reassured us. The kind of reassurance we need now is some evidence and confidence that our governments are making a genuine, all-out effort to solve the UFO mystery and that they will provide us with the truth of their findings. The worldwide, hush-hush UFO policy of the past has only led to a deplorable lack of faith in governmental UFO investigations and the governments concerned can only be held responsible for damaging their own public image in this regard.

As for the University of Toronto UFO investigation group, a rather curious statement was made by Dr. Patterson: "Our point of view is that it is time to look into the whole question of whether technical and other available information on Canadian UFO sightings is being properly collated and assessed. If this is not being done, then there is a chance we would do it in cooperation with the U.S. government, in which case, we'd hope to interest the Canadian government in it, too." It strikes us as a little odd that a Canadian group of scientists should appeal first to the U.S. government for cooperation in its project, and only hope that the Canadian government would become interested. And thus the doubts continue to pile up ever higher.

And so, with uncertainties on both sides of the border, it looks as though we are back to Square One again, with the old diehards, the private UFO research groups, still carrying the ball. But, nil desperandum, we may yet win the game! Reference to the work of UFO groups brings us back to the original subject of this chapter – the chunk of unidentified hardware at Ottawa. During the three-month Colorado silence period, some interesting developments were taking place in Canada. Ronald Anstee, Chairman of the Montreal UFO Society, was, around that time, giving a series of lectures, radio and TV talks on UFO subjects among which was one on the mysterious chunk of hardware at Ottawa. We had already given Ron some samples of the metal during a visit to our club and a few of these were displayed at a lecture he gave to a largish group in Montreal. After his talk, he was approached by a member of the audience who said he was in a position to have the samples thoroughly tested and analyzed by a professional metallurgist friend of his. Ron gladly accepted the offer and by mutual arrangement, it was agreed that, for scientific test purposes, no background details concerning the metal would be given to the analyst. We stress this point because it has a strange bearing on the results obtained. The metallurgist's report follows:

Findings:

1. The corrosion on the part was slight and only superficial.

2. The specific gravity was very high.

3. The hardness was Rockwell B 94.

4. Chemical Analysis

Carbon 0.16%; Manganese 11.3; Sulphur 0.017; NI —; MO—; SI 0.12; FE Ferrous 88.403.

Conclusion

The chemical analysis does not correspond to any commercial manganese steels as they contain either more carbon and silicon or some nickel and molybdenum. The alloy work hardened very heavily during the process of cutting which is inherent to such an alloy. The slipped lines were more pronounced once nital reagent was used. Since deep electro-polishing was used in this instance, it indicates that the material went through heavy impact that caused the different planes to slip.

Comments

1. For a regular manganese steel, the carbon content should be at least 1.6%, not 0.16% and the sulfur should be in the neighborhood of .2%.

2. The fact that this composition does not correspond to any known commercial manganese steel, is, in itself, very interesting, but it does not exclude the possibility of unpublished new materials being used by either the U.S.S.R. or U.S.A.

in their space probes.

3. We can only conjecture regarding the usefulness of the work hardening of the material. Space projectories need material resistant to terrific temperatures and frictions. A material so formulated would indeed help in overcoming these problems.

4. The FE Ferrous percentage of 88.403 may be an erroneous figure since we were unable to make further quality tests, having exhausted the available material.

It is possible there may be an element here that we know nothing about – a most unscientific statement, though.

We would draw your attention to three interesting factors in the above report: (1) The analysis was carried out without prior knowledge of the background details concerning the metal.

(2) The report states in part "...it indicates that the metal went through heavy impact that caused the different planes to slip." We should add here that the report was accompanied by two photomicrographs which show clearly the slipped lines (Newman's lines) in the grains of the metal. Now, if this metal underwent such heavy impact as to cause extensive slippage, surely it is a reasonably logical conclusion that this hardware must have been part of a spacecraft that came to grief – it is hardly conceivable that a foundry product would be subjected to such extreme impact. It is possible, of course, as suggested in the report, that it might have been part of a Russian or American space capsule, but if this were the case, why didn't the Canadian government agency hang on to it? Could it be that, in fact, it was completely unidentifiable and that rather than admit they had proof-positive of a UFO, they preferred to ignore it?

(3) The report states that the metal does not correspond to any known commercial manganese steels and suggests the possibility of an element they know nothing about. This again surely suggests an extraterrestrial metal. In the meantime, the indefatigable Ronald Anstee, still bent on solving the mystery of the metal, had submitted other samples of it for test and analysis by a group of scientists at McGill University in Montreal. A week or so later, he received a telephone call from Professor John Jonas, heading the group, who informed him that the scientists conducting the tests and analyses were "very disturbed" at their findings! He asked for extra samples for further tests. Later, he phoned Ron Anstee again, this time suggesting that the Ottawa New Sciences Club got in touch with a couple of his colleagues, government scientists and experts in metallurgy, whom he thought would be interested in the metal and who had access to more sophisticated equipment than McGill had for testing and analyzing the material.

The necessary contact was made with these two gentlemen and full details, including the latest analysis report, were passed on to them. The two scientists expressed interest in the hardware and on Oct. 14, 1967, arrangements were made for them to examine the mass of metal on site and take samples of it for investigation. Both appeared extremely intrigued by the mysterious circumstances surrounding the finding of the metal and subsequent tests on it. Later, word reached us by telephone that they were prepared to carry out extensive tests and analyses of the samples of metal. It was explained that a thorough analysis was normally rather a long and costly procedure and they were of the opinion that such a comprehensive analysis had not yet been carried out on the metal. However, they were, at the time, working on some new experimental equipment by means of which it was hoped to conduct such an analysis with a great saving in time and money.

Special parts for this equipment were on order from overseas and it was added that delivery of these parts and subsequent testing of the completed apparatus might take anywhere up to six months to complete. However, when it was ready, the necessary investigation would be carried out and a report of the findings sent to us.

With the metal back in government hands again, inevitable doubts arise as to whether the report will be a genuine one, or even if the delaying tactics mentioned above were perhaps an alibi to stall us off for a while. The explanation given us may be quite genuine, but from past experience, we must be excused if we are a little skeptical. However, it must in all fairness be said that the two scientists appeared extremely interested in the metal, genuine in their desire to solve the mystery and they cooperated very willingly. If left to them, we feel we might get a true report. For the time being then, the mystery of the unidentified hardware remains unsolved, although there would now appear to be even stronger indications that the metal may be of extraterrestrial origin.

[Editor's note: In the hundreds of cases in which flying saucer occupants have been sighted there have been almost as many differing descriptions of these "humanoids." A complete analysis of this aspect of the UFO phenomena has been undertaken by the present editor of Topside, Mrs. Carol Halford-Watkins.

Her conclusions and comments are quite interesting in light of the research being done by such important researchers as John A. Keel, Lucius Farish, Jerome Clark, Dr. Jacques Vallee and others. T.G.B.]

Top: The mysterious chunk of metal as photographed in a Canadian government laboratory where it underwent a limited amount of tests and analyses by the late Wilbert B. Smith. The white lines shown on the metal were placed there by WBS for identification purposes.

Bottom: Shows one of the inclusions on the outer surface of the metal taken with the aid of microphotography.

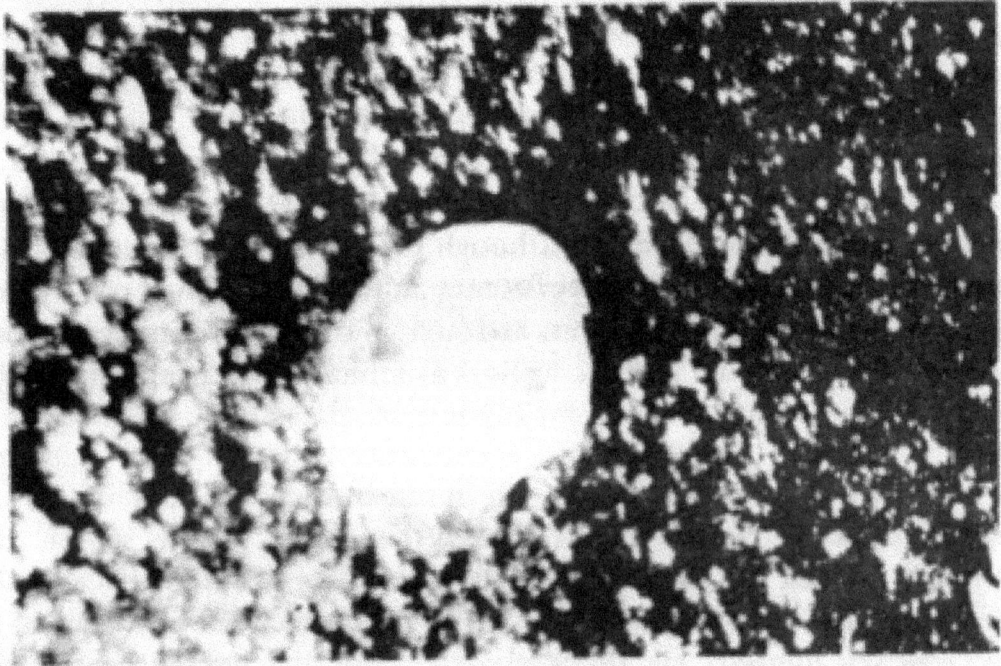

THE CASE FOR THE HUMANOIDS

I don't think you will locate the word "humanoid" in the dictionary, although undoubtedly it will find its way there in due course. This deftly-coined word is strictly a product of the UFO Age and it was invented as an apt and necessary measure with which to compare the extraterrestrial beings of a similar biological structure to ourselves, as reported to have been seen by many witnesses as the landed occupants of UFOs, with the basic physical characteristics of homo sapiens on earth.

While much of the data on which this article is based was obtained from various books, magazines and newspaper articles containing reports of alleged contacts with humanoid occupants of landed alien spacecraft, its main source of information has been from an excellent booklet on the subject put out by "Flying Saucer Review" under the title of "The Humanoids: A Survey of Worldwide Reports of Landings of Unconventional Aerial Objects and their Alleged Occupants".

As it is not the intention of the writer to list complete details of these individual reports, it is suggested that any readers who may be seriously interested in the humanoids story should obtain a copy of "The Humanoids," study the wealth of data given, the views expressed by well-known UFO writers, and then form their own conclusions. This booklet may be obtained from "Flying Saucer Review," 21 Cecil Court, Charing Cross Road, London, W.C.2., England, for $1.75 remittance payable to "Flying Saucer Review." It is well worth reading.

Rather, the purpose of this article is to study the humanoids en masse, analyze the various reports, to seek any pattern or possible relationship between them and to put forward a few suggested hypotheses for these strange phenomena. Let us then first study the humanoids en masse—and what a queer, motley crew they make, ranging from midgets to giants, from esthetic, Christ-like creatures to horrific monsters! At first glance, if we are to believe these reports, we might well be tempted to conclude that all the many races of the entire universe are visiting planet Earth! Of course, certain climatic and environmental conditions on other planets could well produce certain variations in the humanoid form, even as on our own planet we have our mongoloid, Negroid, Caucasian and other ethnic groups, but whereas all earth races have the same biological features in common, i.e., two eyes, two ears, one mouth, one nose, two arms, two legs, etc., the wide divergence from this orderly theme of human construction as described by some witnesses of humanoids, such as mouthless, nose-less, having one or three eyes, fingers with no thumbs, etc., make it appear doubtful that all of these creatures belong strictly to the humanoid race at all. To give our readers a clearer picture of what is involved and omitting here those humanoids described as basically the same as ourselves, let us run a checklist down some of the major physical features of man on earth and compare them with those of some of the humanoids as described in published accounts:

Head: "large, high, pointed head with facial features low down," "large," "huge," "large, with high forehead," "round and bald," "extremely round," "oval with pointed ears," "pointed," "tapered at top," "white-domed," "melon-shaped," "pumpkin-like," "a flattened ball," "large and round, with very long ears," "painted-on hair effect looking like rolls of fat running from above eyes over the whole head," "gnome-like, with huge elephant ears," "pear-shaped, with bulbous portion on top."

Analysis: The "Big Heads" seem to have it, with "Long Ears" running a close second! Egg "long," "round," "oval-shaped," "triangular," "Oriental," "high cheek boned," "Mongolian," "Chinese-looking," "pointed chin," "very pointed chin," "red, with sharply pointed chin," "hairy," "hair-covered," "sparsely bearded," "mouthless," "no ears or nose," "shriveled," "furrowed," "pasty-white," "putty-colored," "frog-like."

Analysis: Composite picture seems to favor a hairy, Mongoloid face, with chin.

Complexion: "pallid," "extremely pale," "fair," "yellow," "sallow," "grey," "of greyish metallic cast," "waxy," "yellowish-green," "green," "light brown," "brownish," "tanned," "reddish-brown," "reddish-orange," "blood red," "vivid red," "just like wax."

Analysis: Predominantly, a waxy red complexion.

Hair: "bald," "totally bald," "long," "short," "shaggy," "long, silky black," "agindant black," "red," "brown," "mousy," "sandy," "blonde," "long and white," "streaming fair hair," "long and blonde."

Analysis: Of these descriptions, the long-haired blonde seems favorite.

Eyes: Eyes come in ones, twos, threes or multi: (1) "One eye, Cyclops fashion, in middle of forehead," "single golden-colored eye, with other smaller eyes up and down body"(!), "one large brown eye." (2) Most descriptions are of two eyes as listed below; (3) "Three eyes staring fixedly, without blinking." Eyes in pairs: "glowing," "large and luminous," "larger than human," "large as a raven's egg," "large and slanted," "huge and set wide apart," "glowing with an orange

88

light," "glowing greenish orange," "glowing yellowish orange," "big and red," "blue," "very blue," "vivid blue, Chinese type," "violet," "plum-colored," "dark brown," "grey like stone," "muddy," "protruding," "protuberant and frog-like," "deep-set," "side-spaced and deep sunk," "wide, slit eyes," "moon-eyed," "yellow cat's eyes."

Analysis: The prevailing picture seems to be large, glowing, slanted, orange eyes.

Nose: "long," "very long," "large and long," "straight and long," "squat," "blob," "two slits for nostrils," "beak-like," "arrangement of four diamond-shaped things where nose should be," "indeterminate," and "no nose at all."

Analysis: Odds-on favorite – long nose.

Mouth: "big and red," "drop-open, making rectangular hole in face," "thin line going across smooth face," "slit-like, extending from ear to ear, barely discernible," "none."

Analysis: Long slit-mouth.

Body: "hairy," "abundant hair," "fur-covered," "hairy and dwarflike," "blinking blue lights on chest," "bulky," "bristly," "large," "strong," "dwarflike," "slimly built," "broad shouldered," "black and resembling a shrub," "lopsided and abnormally large on right side, bulging from shoulder to armpit," "barrel-like, with side to side waddle"(!)

Analysis: The only possible picture that emerges is a sort of deformed King Kong.

Hands: "clammy," "white," "green, claw-like, with 8 fingers," "webbed extremities with claws," "4 even-length, spread-out fingers with no thumb," "square," "rectangular," "globular," "huge talons," "outsized webbed hands equipped with claws," "no hands."

Analysis: Claw-like.

Arms: "unusually long," "long and thin, with claw-like appendages," "arms with metal plates attached and numerous small lights," "one arm longer than other," "very long and ending in claws."

Analysis: Long and clawed.

Legs: "stiff-gaited," "thin," "short and thin," "longer than human," "long and slender."

Analysis: Long, thin legs.

Voice: "definitely human," "high pitched," "Chinese-sounding," "guttural," "chattering," "like cackling of geese," "pipe-like, sounding like a kazoo," "clacking," "hooting," "cooing" and "unintelligible."

Analysis: Take your choice!

Height: 2'6", 3', 3'6", 4'6", 4'8", 5'4", 5'5", 5'8", 6', 6'8", 7', 10', 10-15'(!) 70cm,

PROJECT MAGNET

80cm, 90cm, 1M, 1.2M, 1.25M, 1.30M, 1.60M, 2M, 2.10M, 5M, 6M!

Analysis: Math was never my strong point, but when I'm asked to visualize beings ranging from under 30" high to about 20' tall, my mind just boggles!

Clothing: "diving gear," "coveralls (in all shades)," "silver suits which rustled like tinfoil," "shiny suit, like glass," "one-piece garb with boots attached," "suit of armor," "rubber overalls," "luminous suit," "metallic diving suit," "garments like plastic bags," "potato sacks," "black sack like a cassock," "transparent suits inflated like rubber bags," "one-piece garment resembling suede, with zippers," "loincloths," "white robes," "yellow sacks," "plastic diver's suit," "greenish one-piece suits, close-fitting at neck, wrists and ankles," "dark grey suits glued to bodies," "green phosphorescent diver's suit," "brown leather diver's suit, with gauntlets," "shining, violet-colored garments," "seamless, 1-piece garments of metallic and unknown fibers," "white clothing emitting flashes of light," "grey tights," "baggy trousers," "ghostlike and lit by internal source," "black, skintight suit, material from thighs down glistening as though wet," "shiny, nickel-plated suit." Helmets: "with pale green lights each side," "with antenna," "translucent and connected by tubing to gear on back," "football," "crash," "transparent," "glass-like," "inverted glass bowl," "with instruments giving off colored flashes," "with two cables linked to spacecraft," "gas masks," "luminous haloes"(!)

Analysis: Above list reads like an invitation to a Halloween Party! However, the typical spaceman's "diver's" suit, with helmet, seems to emerge prominently.

* * * * *

There you have the descriptive details, all taken from published reports. Confused? You should be. I am, too. But, in the words of a famous comedian: "You ain't heard nuthin' yet!" Dig this crazy composite picture of a humanoid based on deductions from the reports given: A big-headed, long-eared, hairy-faced Mongol-type, with pointed chin, large, glowing orange eyes, long nose, long slit mouth, red apple complexion and long blonde hair falling to gorilla-like body, with long arms ending in claws and long thin legs!

And if this doesn't strike you as funny-peculiar, how about this one? Jerry Townsend's Tin Men, whom he described as: "Three little beer-can shaped objects, 6" high, that walked on two fins and when they stopped, a third fin came down from the rear."(!) Could Jerry have been watching too many TV commercials? More seriously, I think the answer for this one is that the objects were not "men" but remotely-controlled monitoring devices operating from a landed UFO. But to add further to the general confusion, a number of scientists, apparently for the lack of a more rational explanation, are now theorizing that the UFOs themselves are space animals, living organisms of a "low order of intelligence" that inhabit the atmosphere and live on cosmic energy.

They even go so far as to interpret the oft-reported cigar-shaped mother ships releasing the smaller scout discs as a space animal giving birth to offspring! Strange how such "alibis" are so often more fantastic than the simple truth. And are our Earth scientists so egotistical that they cannot accept the possibility of extraterrestrial intelligence superior to their own? Personally, I cannot buy this theory that the UFOs themselves are organic creatures and particularly of a "low order of intelligence." This is far removed from the vast majority of reputable reports that UFOs are spacecraft of superior technology under the highly intelligent control of space beings, many of whom have been actually seen.

Nevertheless, it does seem that the more we dig into this puzzling enigma, the more complex and inexplicable it all becomes. For example, I began this article in a serious enough vein, hoping to arrive at a few intelligent conclusions from my analysis of the reports, but the more I read, the more ludicrous it all sounded and all I wound up with was a lot of laughs and some big fat questions, such as: Who's kidding whom? Are some of these reports bordering on the lunatic fringe? Could some of these apparitions be the work of poltergeists or astral entities? Are we being made the victims of some great cosmic joke? Are some of our human observers being hypnotized or hallucinated into seeing such grotesque figures? Could the whole range of peculiar shapes and sizes be a deliberate disguise to cover up the true identity of the extraterrestrials? One could go on and on asking questions of a complex situation like this.

But let us take a final and more serious look at the Humanoids as far as we can know them from earthly descriptions. On the one hand, we have the Adamski-type Venusians described as having a pleasant, round face, with high forehead, calm, grey eyes slightly aslant at the corners, finely chiseled nose, average sized mouth, complexion medium-colored suntan, slender hands with long, tapering fingers, wavy, shoulder-length hair of a glistening sand color and about 5'6" in height. In short, beings very much like ourselves in physical appearance but more spiritually evolved. These I can believe in – and from a personal experience – so this is not just idealistic, wishful thinking. To me, it seems quite logical that the Deity, having created a functional physical body such as we inhabit on earth, should extend this same biological structure to human-type life on the estimated millions of other planets similar to our own, even allowing for a few minor physical changes brought about by different environmental conditions. If we are to believe the Bible, God created Man in His own image, and as all life is created by the same Divine Intelligence, it seems reasonable to assume that the same basic physical form would be given to all human-type races in the universe.

On the other hand, the composite picture of the humanoids en masse presents a fantastic and somewhat frightening spectacle to the earthly eye. Even allowing for a reasonable amount of superficial differences, if a being is basically the human animal, why do such grotesque peculiarities exist among them? The human body, in a normal, healthy person, is a near-perfect biological mechanism in which no superfluous function exists and nothing important has been omitted for the survival of the species. Why is it, then, that descriptions of humanoids include such inexplicable differences which are not compatible with the efficient functioning of the human-type body?

One of these differences I am unable to accept as the logical outcome of a Divine Creator is a humanoid with 4 fingers and no thumb. As we all must know, a thumb, along with 4 or even more fingers, is an all-necessary appendage without which we would be unable to perform most of the useful and creative manual functions. Having once sprained my right thumb, I am well aware of its utilitarian importance! Equally, the human mind cannot possibly conceive the purpose or even the physical relationship in a humanoid body, with presumably a central nervous system connected to the brain, of one eye, three eyes and still less, multi eyes!

Why then do all these strange differences continually crop up in an ever widening variety in so many reports of the occupants of alien spacecraft? Perhaps the answer is to be found in the interpretation of what the witnesses actually saw. While not discounting the claim that these observers did experience a physical encounter with landed extraterrestrials, is it not possible that they underwent some psychological compulsion, possibly at the subconscious level, to include these "differences" as frills to be interpreted as proof positive that they had indeed contacted alien beings from another planet? Another interesting theory put forward in the Introduction to "The Humanoids" is that the extremely varied descriptions of UFOs and their occupants may be due in some way to the "environment" of the witness, i.e., that what he sees is "in the eye of the beholder." One might be inclined to go along with this theory, as it is an interesting fact that most of the more grotesque descriptions of humanoids come from ill-educated peasants and farmers in the rural areas of South America, France, etc., people with an understandably limited outlook.

In contrast, men with wider horizons, such as Wilbert B. Smith, George Adamski and quite a few others, have described our space visitors as being built in the same shape as ourselves, but more advanced mentally and spiritually. Of course, this may be an oversimplification which does not cover the whole humanoid story. For instance, some reports include descriptions of dwarfs who appear to be robots under the mental control of the humanoids proper and who perform limited tasks on Earth, such as collecting samples of water, soil, minerals, plants, and even small animals (a farmer in Isola, Italy, claimed such a dwarf immobilized him and stole his rabbits). We might theorize that these robots evolve from two possible sources: 1) They are the natural inhabitants of a more backward planet whose subnormal mentality is susceptible to "brainwashing" and submission to the will of more advanced beings from another planet; or 2) They are artificially-created beings with no real will power of their own who respond mechanically to the wishes of their creators. A number of reports indicate that such landed dwarfs work under the control of a taller being seen in the spacecraft. Apparently, although immensely strong for their size, these dwarfs never use their strength to harm humans. If it becomes necessary to defend themselves, according to a number of reports, they use a ray or vapor gas ejected from a belt or chest contraption which temporarily paralyzes any human interfering with its activities. As for the few reports of giants and monsters, while open-minded, I am more inclined to write these off as figments of the observer's imagination.

From analytical deductions based on such evidence as we have, we seem to have broken down our original heterogeneous collection of humanoids into 4 major categories: 1) beings physically very much like ourselves; 2) humanoids sharing many of our physical characteristics but with certain inexplicable differences; 3) dwarf-robots apparently masterminded by the humanoids; and 4) a small sprinkling of doubtful giants and monsters. What does all this add up to? Groping in the dark and with so many pieces of the jigsaw puzzle missing, we can only theorize. Undoubtedly, time will add more pieces to the puzzle and the full picture will gradually emerge. But for now, we can only sum up as follows: Out of an estimated 1000 reported contacts with humanoids over the past 20 years, many from reputable sources, it is reasonable to assume that at least 25% of the claims are genuine; actually it would only take 1% to prove the case for the humanoids.

Whether all the physical descriptions are accurate is a debatable question, but there is good evidence to believe that various types of extraterrestrials are actually landing on earth. From most accounts, it appears that humanoid encounters with earthlings are purely accidental, i.e., humans stumble on the scene of their landing and, usually, the extraterrestrials take off at speed shortly after the confrontation, presumably not wishing to tangle with that aggressive species, homo sapiens, against whom, in self-defense, they might have to use weapons of superior technology! This may well be the key to the mystery of lack of contact. The fault lies in earthman's own aggressive nature. If and when the day finally dawns that we can, in vast numbers, welcome our space visitors with genuine friendliness, there may then be a valuable exchange of scientific and cultural ideas between us and our brothers in space.

PROJECT MAGNET

UFO OCCUPANTS AND CRITTERS
INTERSECTIONS WITH JOHN BRENT MUSGRAVE

Intersections with John Musgrave, on learning from his Colombian-born wife, Consuelo, of his sudden death of a heart attack August 11, 2015 (by Richard Gordon).

I met John probably in my last year of high school at the University of Chicago Laboratory School. He was then an undergraduate at the University of Chicago, and a member of the Astronomy Club (still in business). The president, Tom, was the older brother of a girl who was a year ahead of me in the Lab School. Tom made me recite some constellations (a difficult task for me, allergic to memorizations) to join the club. I learned them once and promptly forgot most, though Big and Little Dippers, Cassiopeia and Orion still stick. By the time I entered UC in 1959 as a 16-year-old student, skipping the senior year in high school, John was President, I became Treasurer, and there were no other members and no membership fees. It was typical of John's wry humor, which I went along with, that he gave me this null responsibility for all our money. I enjoyed the irony.

John lived in the crawl space between the roof and the ceiling, just high enough to sit up on the mattress he set up in there, above our club room atop the Ryerson Physics Building, accessed by a narrow helical staircase. John kept his personal belongings locked in the club room, explaining that the purpose of locks was to keep honest people honest. Above the club room, from which we could look east across the campus, was the observatory on the roof containing a 6 inch refracting telescope. Daytimes I would occasionally sketch projected images of the sun's spots. At night I sometimes brought a date up there. I tried simultaneously photographing the same meteorites with my brother, with him at our home in southwest Chicago and me at UC. I had built a strobing device consisting of a fan blade on a motor that went in front of the camera, so that the images of meteorites would be a sequence of dashes, allowing calculation of their velocity But the film cracked in the cold of night when advanced in the camera, and I didn't think about how to overcome that problem. Dan later became an excellent amateur astronomer with his own observatory, and a prize winning astronomy photographer. He still volunteers at McDonald Observatory in Texas.

Astronomy overnights with John meant we played with an ancient brass calculating machine we had, listened to classical music on WFMT (a radio station still on, now available on Internet), and browsed through negatives of galaxies photographed by previous members. That space became my second campus home, my first being my own lab over the central lecture theater in the Kent Chemistry Building, where I kept a cot and cooked canned spaghetti in a beaker. I prepared specimens for students to analyze for the quantitative chemistry course, after taking that course my first summer before I entered UC. Ed Anders taught it. I later worked with him on organic matter in meteors.

John majored in history of science, and via him I gained an appreciation for that history. I recall sitting in on a course on modelling in science, undoubtedly because of John. John questioned everything, especially having to do with authority, and I owe much of my professional and daily skepticism to discussions with him. He told me about Vulcan, the planet deduced from its perturbations of Mercury's orbit, and that was sometimes observed, between Mercury and the sun. It was later explained away by relativistic effects on Mercury's orbit. We discussed phenomena such as people seeing lights on the Moon. John told me that when he was a kid, in broad daylight he used his telescope to watch something in the sky that had parts twirling around and going in and out, unlike any aircraft with which he was familiar. He later wrote a short book on UFO sightings in Canada. Again, I learned from him open-mindedness about things, raising questions, but not jumping to conclusions based on scant evidence. He was not a believer in UFOs, just open to their possibility. After a visit five years ago that Natalie and I paid to the UFO museum in Roswell, New Mexico, I made sure they got a copy of his book into their extensive library.

John came to my home, where my parents, Jack and Diana Gordon, got to know and like him. This probably made it easier on them when at 17 I moved out and shared an apartment with John and one other fellow in Hyde Park, north of the University. He also got to know George and Susan Meschel. Susan was a grad student in Quantitative Chemistry, who along with Jim Dwyer looked after me. I was younger than everyone else in my class, so it was these people, along with Helmut Hirsch and later Victor Fried, a prodigy in Biophysics, also my age, who formed my world.

I went off to graduate school at age 19 to the Institute for Molecular Biology at the University of Oregon. John's pacifism wore off on me: "Do you believe in the use of force? Well, I do use a can opener." Always a wry point of view. At UO I was kept out of the army draft "in the national interest" and joined many of the discussions pro and con about the Vietnam War. But this is John's story.

PROJECT MAGNET

John visited me once in Oregon, driving up from California, where his parents lived. His father, a laborer as I recalled, in the San Diego area, had done a lot of reading on witchcraft, which influenced John. (My father, a home remodeling salesman, was likewise a collector of all books on Franklin D. Roosevelt.) On a visit to John down there, he made a remark about my moustache looking like Hitler's. When I mentioned this to him 50 years later, he said it showed how cruel kids can be to one another. The bad memory was laid to rest. In retrospect his remark was just his observation of the incongruity of a Jew bearing such a moustache. Although not Jewish himself, he did observe that most of his friends were Jewish.

On one visit John and I drove to and stayed with an old friend of his, who lived on the coast of northern Oregon. We caught razor clams on the beach, overcoming their amazing speed through sand with a half meter long sheet metal pipe capped at one end to let air out, with thumb over the hole to pull out a core of sand with clam. His friend couldn't pay the taxes on his tiny home, so it went up for auction, and he bought it. More wryness.

For a year or two I kept a diary of sorts in the form of long, handwritten letters to John. Unfortunately, in his wanderings he had to lighten his load, and they were gone.

John collected books, amassing over 3000 of them, for which Consuelo now needs a buyer. He had rare books of interest to historians of science, and an eclectic variety of others. When I sold mine to begin full time RVing with Natalie, I had only 2000 to my name, much the same in kind, but focusing on biology instead of physics and astronomy. He moved to Edmonton, was in graduate school at the University of Alberta for a while, and I visited him there with his newly wed Consuelo, our young sons Chason and Justin in tow. When later he was short of cash, I bought a shelf of books from him on religion and science.

Natalie and I visited John and Consuelo during our two stays in Osoyoos, British Columbia, winter 2013/14, seeing them at their home in Oliver and in restaurants. I attended a meeting of the local historical society with John. He was much the same, but had drifted far from science, the two of them having fostered many First Nations kids, and he getting involved in the history of local First Nations affairs. The last I saw him was when he came to our RV camp site (run by the Osoyoos Indian Band with whom John worked) to try to help me with a bolt on our trailer hitch, which would not budge with the tools we had between us.

John was one of those fine intellects who could never have made it in academia. I squeaked through, despite the attitudes I learned from John and concurred with. In retrospect, though I didn't think of him that way, he was a fine, exemplary big brother. I'm off shortly to a conference on the origin of life, where I will be trying to tempt people to join me in a book on The Habitability of the

Universe Before Earth, which if it comes to fruition will be dedicated to John's memory.

Some of John's Publications:

Musgrave, J.B. (1979). UFO Occupants & Critters: The Patterns in Canada. New York, Global Communications.

Musgrave, J.B. & J. Houran (2000). Flight and abduction in witchcraft and UFO lore. Psychological Reports 86(2), 669-688

Musgrave, J.B. & J. Houran (2003). The Witches' Sabbat in legend and literature. Lore and Language 17, 157

Musgrave, J.B. (2003). Smallpox as a weapon of genocide in the Okanagan and Similkameen? Report of the Okanagan Historical Society 67, 41-43.

Entity as drawn by Witness.

Entity as Drawn by Barney Hill.

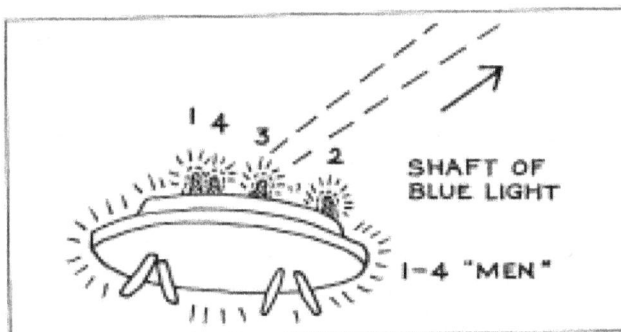

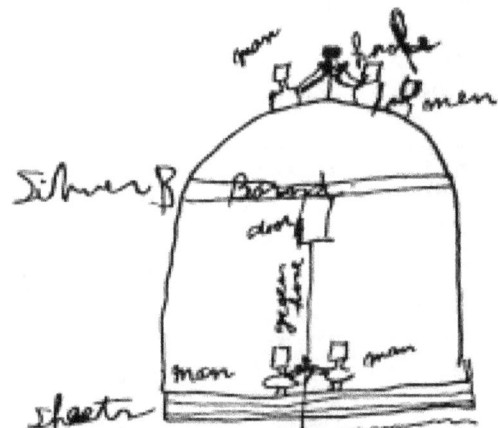

UFO and Entities Drawn by William Kiehl

PROJECT MAGNET

PREFACE

As part of their Explorations Program, the Canada Council awarded me a grant in 1975 to help prepare a book on the history of the UFO phenomenon across Canada. The purpose of this proposed work was, and is, at least twofold: to document the social history of a phenomenon, and to collect as many UFO case histories, past and present, that have been reported in Canada. This small book is in part a progress report on one kind of case history being collected for this on-going project.

This work would have been impossible without the cooperation of the many individuals and UFO groups who have shared their files and findings with me, either personally or through their publications. Most collections of original sighting reports from Canada are now located in the files of major UFO organizations based in the United States. For this work, I've particularly made use of the material on file with the Aerial Phenomena Research Organization in Tucson, Arizona, the Center for UFO Studies, in Evanston, Illinois, and the National Investigations Committee on Aerial Phenomena, in Kensington, Maryland. I'd particularly like to express my appreciation for the assistance of Shelia Kudrle, Coral Lorenzen, and Jim Lorenzen of APRO; and J. Allen Hynek and Margo Metegrano of the CUFOS.

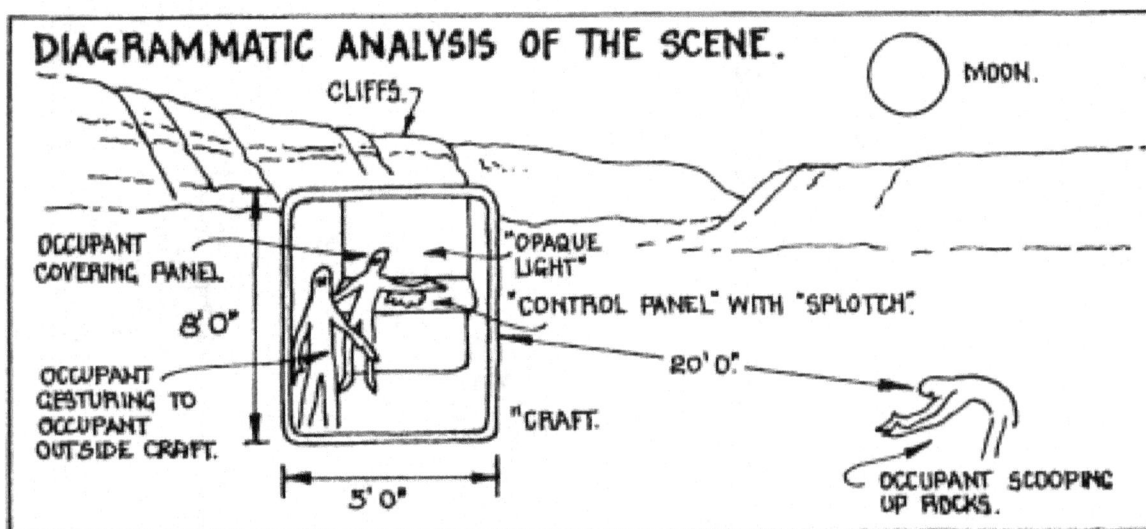

DIAGRAMMATIC ANALYSIS OF THE SCENE.

CLIFFS.

MOON.

OCCUPANT COVERING PANEL.

"OPAQUE LIGHT"

"CONTROL PANEL" WITH "SPLOTCH".

8' 0"

OCCUPANT GESTURING TO OCCUPANT OUTSIDE CRAFT.

20' 0"

"CRAFT."

OCCUPANT SCOOPING UP ROCKS.

5' 0"

PROJECT MAGNET

THE UFO AND EXTRATERRESTRIALS
WHAT'S A UFO?

There is no universal agreement of just what makes up a UFO report or a UFO. In the popular press, the term is often used interchangeably to mean a "flying saucer" or spaceship. For better, and mostly worse, many of the ideas and controversies surrounding this phenomenon, as well as the popular understanding about it, has been generated by the extraterrestrial connection. (1) All too often members of the scientific community are called on to make statements about UFO reports, even though they often know little about the subject except that somehow it's connected in popular culture with mystical and occult ideas. There are in fact some studies which have attempted to be scientific in their approach to this phenomenon, and one of their first tasks is to make some working definition. The controversial Condon committee made one definition of a UFO that has also been used by other investigators. (2) According to this definition:

"...an unidentified flying object (UFO, pronounced OOFO) is here defined as the stimulus for a report made by one or more individuals of something seen in the sky (or an object thought to be capable of flight but seen when landed on the earth) which the observer could not identify as having an ordinary natural origin, and which seemed to him sufficiently puzzling that he undertook to make a report of it to police, to government officials, to the press, or perhaps to a representative of a private organization devoted to the study of such objects."

Defined in this way, there is no question that UFO reports exist in large numbers. And defined in this way, there is no question that many of these reports are generated by a great number of different things going on in the real world that may seem strange to the witness, but which have a mundane, even if interesting, explanation. The definition is consciously broad, and there seems to be no reason why it couldn't be a useful starting off point. However, the manner in which this definition came to be used by Dr. Condon and others led Dr. J. Allen Hynek to suggest an amended version: (3)

"We can define the UFO simply as the reported perception of an object or light seen in the sky or upon the land the appearance, trajectory, and general dynamic and luminescent behavior of which is not only mystifying to the original percipients but remains unidentified after close scrutiny of all available evidence by persons who are technically capable of making a common sense identification, if one is possible."

This definition rules out the greater percentage of UFO cases as defined by the Condon report (e.g., the planet Venus, fireballs, weather balloons, etc.). (4) And this definition implies that some UFO reports are in fact generated by new, as yet unrecognized, phenomenon going on in the real world. For this reason, it's the kind of definition many UFO researchers prefer, and the one implicit in this work.

Tales of unusual events have interested man since the dawn of time.

Charles Fort at the beginning of this century was continuing a tradition that was old even two thousand years ago when Pliny collected tales of fantastic beasties and weird lights and apparitions in the sky. Many of these ancient reports have turned out to be accounts of natural phenomena which later could be given a scientific explanation. And many of the contemporary reports of strange lights in the sky will prove to also have scientific explanations. While many of these explanations are already known, it's the contention of most UFO researchers that some of them are yet to be explained. In this view, at least some UFO reports are in fact potential clues to new scientific discoveries. It should be kept in mind that they are potential clues to discoveries – empirical data – and they are not a science in their own right.

While Dr. Condon suggests that no scientific information has been gained so far from the study of UFOs, and implies that none ever will, (5) he does cover himself on this point by stating: "Although we conclude, after nearly two years of intensive study, that we do not see any fruitful lines of advance from the study of UFO reports, we believe that any scientist with adequate training and credentials who does come up with a clearly defined, specific proposal for study should be supported."

It's highly unlikely, however, that funds ever will be given for UFO research if such research is defined as a discipline in its own right. While there may be a UFO phenomenon that can be studied by historians, sociologists, psychologists and other social scientists, the UFO reports themselves are generated by a wide variety of physical phenomenon with no particular scientific correlation or connection. One of the many difficulties and muddles with so-called UFO research is that in fact we are dealing with a wide variety of quite unique events going on in the real world. All they may have in common is the fact that they are as yet unidentified, and gave off a light. Hardly a scientific correlation. Although many researchers have given lip service to this elementary fact, in practice they often ignore it.

Other than proposals for creating information banks, it seems unlikely that funds ever will, or should, be devoted to UFO research, other than those projects which are interested in it as a social phenomenon. This doesn't mean that UFO reports aren't of potential scientific interest. The fact of the matter is that studies have been and are being funded for research that could benefit by the knowledge of some of the reports that have been collected and filed under the ubiquitous term UFO. If there is in fact a phenomenon of ball lightning (6), some UFO reports are unquestionably due to this phenomenon. Even though one may disagree with the number of UFO cases that can be explained as ball lightning, the work of Philip Klass and others is an important contribution in drawing attention to the UFO research community this category of phenomenon. (7) Similarly, if earthquake lightning does in fact exist – that is, if prior to major earthquakes in certain parts of the world luminous lights are sometimes seen in the sky – then some UFO reports are likely occurrences of this unusual phenomenon. (8) As such they could prove to be useful public precursors of earthquakes. A recent paper has even suggested that a correlation of UFO sightings with spruce budworm infections might give some insight into nocturnal insect flight patterns. (9) These, and other studies, could in fact benefit if UFO reports were taken more seriously and collected in a fashion and form that would make them accessible to scientists.

Unfortunately, this has never been done. Usually the UFO phenomenon has been introduced to scientists in the context of science vs. the occult. And on that basis they have attacked it as they would any mystical and unscientific world view that pretended to be scientific. Usually they have gone about their attack on the UFO phenomenon without investigating and finding out what research, ideas and findings have been made – many by scientists who have established a reputation in traditional scientific fields. Some members of the scientific community have gone further than this. Some have used the UFO as a vehicle to attack and slander ordinary people. Rather than interpret the wide-scale misunderstanding of science in general, and the UFO phenomenon in particular, as a criticism of the educational (and by inference the social and political) system, they use it to attack the fundamental nature and integrity of people. A recent article by a Canadian astronomer, who also happens to be in charge of the UFO files at the National Research Council in Ottawa, and who stated on a national CBC radio show that he didn't believe in UFOs, "because he didn't believe in little green men," illustrates this fascist, and fundamentally unscientific view of man: (10) "The human basically believes what he wants to believe and sees what he wants to see .... In a continued deluge of ideas from the public media of newspapers, radio and TV, the individual loses his capacity for individual reason and follows the flock..."

As long as people who have this view of the nature of man (and how could science have ever been developed if people were really like this), and the nature of the UFO phenomenon, are in control of UFO reports and influence the official policy of how to deal with UFO reports, a potentially useful reservoir of data will remain hidden to other scientists.

PROJECT MAGNET

THE EXTRATERRESTRIAL CONNECTION

The Condon study was made within the intellectual framework of the extra-terrestrial origin of UFO reports. While this idea enjoyed great popular support, it was one that Drs. Hynek and Jacque Vallee, among others, strongly urged the committee to abandon. Both men had been involved with the phenomenon for many years. Hynek as scientific consultant to the U.S. Air Force, and Vallee as a scientist who had his own experience with UFOs as well as the experience of writing two books on the subject. They argued that the ETH (Extraterrestrial Hypothesis) should be thought of as just one of many possible explanations. But Condon, and some of the other members of the committee, insisted that a major portion of the project be an attempt to prove or disprove the alien origin of UFOs. (2) This not only led to dissatisfaction and discord within the Condon committee, but also led ultimately to the judgement of the reality and worth of empirical data being made on the basis of whether or not a particular hypothesis or explanation of that empirical data proved to be tenable or not. It's as if an astronomer were to reject the existence of lunar eclipses because he isn't willing to accept that dragons can eat up the moon. Already by the time of the Condon committee, many scientists who had looked at the UFO reports had come to the conclusion that these reports represented useful data, but that they didn't support the ETH hypothesis.

The Condon committee missed an excellent opportunity of weeding out ex-traneous, and often mystical and unscientific, speculation about a set of observations from the observations themselves. Instead they chose to throw out both the observations and the speculations. It may be irrelevant whether this was a con-scious decision or not. But it is not irrelevant that even though approximately 30% of the cases the committee investigated were still unidentified at the end of the study, there never was an attempt to analyze what patterns, if any, existed in these UFO reports. In many ways the Condon report had an effect opposite to the one desired by its authors – it even more closely welded the idea that UFOs are extra-terrestrial in origin. It placed many people in a kind of dilemma. They were con-vinced, even after consulting with "experts," that they had experienced some-thing quite real and unusual, and that all explanations they could think of didn't explain what they saw. The effect of the kind of view expressed in the Condon report was to intimate that anyone who saw a UFO either didn't know Jupiter from a flashlight, or ought to change brands, or ought to see an analyst. Given the choice, many chose to accept the reality of their sighting, and by inference, the explana-tion that it must have been a "spaceship."

Such episodes have led some to lose faith in the abilities of scientists and in the scientific method. From the perspective of one who is in continual touch with UFO witnesses, and who is also trained in both the physical and social sciences,

I've found it ironic and deplorable that the authoritarian manner in which some scientists have dismissed all UFO reports as nonsense has in fact contributed to a distrust in science. It is a major concern which is often neglected by scientists and educators. (12)

The idea that life exists elsewhere in the universe is as old as man. Some of the earliest literature revolves around the creation myth, and many of these stories are connected with angels, teachers from the skies, and similar celestial visitors. In Greek times, the idea of the plurality of worlds was closely associated with, and formed the core of, the ancient atomist or materialist philosophy of Leucippus and Democritus, and their Roman successors Epicurus and Lucretius. The idea that life existed elsewhere in the universe was considered a heresy by the Church, which regarded creation as both Divine and unique. Scientific martyrs, such as Bruno, were burned at the stake not so much for teaching the Copernican cosmology that said the earth is just one of many planets going around the sun, as for believing in the plurality of worlds. This idea was again closely connected with the revival of the materialist viewpoint of the atomists, and was connected to the thinking that led to the scientific revolution. (13)

By the end of the nineteenth century and the beginning of the twentieth, the idea that many worlds are inhabited was commonly accepted among educated laymen if not among all scientists. In 1903, for instance, Alfred Russel Wallace could argue in "Man's Place in the Universe" that the modern belief in other worlds was: "...founded more upon religious ideas than upon a scientific and careful examination of the whole of the facts both astronomical, physical, and biological, and we must agree with the late Dr. Whewell, that the belief that other planets are inhabited has been greatly entertained, not in consequence of the physical reasons but in spite of them."

Other scientists, most notably Percival Lowell, believed not only that in theory life could exist elsewhere in the universe, but that there were actual signs of its existence nearby on the surface of the planet Mars. In 1877, the Italian astronomer Giovanni Schiaparelli had observed fine lines crossing the planet Mars. His term for these markings was translated into English as "canals" and with it the implication of intelligent creation. Most astronomers never saw these markings, but Lowell was one who often observed them through the 24-inch telescope at Flagstaff, Arizona. And he believed them to in fact be the remains of ancient Martian civilizations who built them as gigantic irrigation networks to water a dry and dying planet. Few other astronomers shared Lowell's views on Mars. But these thoughts were reflected in the literature of the time. In this context, it may prove significant that the most famous novel of that time that discussed life on Mars was H. G. Wells' "The War of the Worlds," which came out as a book in 1898, and which was illustrated with Martian ships that look very much like modern drawings of UFOs with legs.

PROJECT MAGNET

About the time Wallace's book appeared, a new scientific theory on the formation of the solar system seemed to collaborate his contention that life was probably unique to planet earth. In 1900 the astronomer F. R. Moulton, and the geologist T. C. Chamberlin proposed the "planetesimal hypothesis" to account for the creation of the solar system. According to this hypothesis, the solar system was created in a spiral nebula which itself was generated by the close approach of two stars. This was proposed as an alternate explanation to the nebular hypothesis which suggested that the solar system was created from the internal collapse of a giant cloud of gas and dust. If solar systems – planets and their parent stars – were in fact created out of infrequent near collisions of stars, planetary formation would be an extremely rare thing in the universe. And the chance of finding life elsewhere remote.

In recent years, however, this hypothesis has given way to more advanced versions of the nebular hypothesis, and scientific wisdom now suggests that life not only is possible on other star system planets, but our understanding of the chemical reactions involved in the creation of life make it likely that such life is rather common. A commonly formulated equation summarizes the probable number of technological civilizations in any galaxy as:

$$N = R\, f_p\, n_e\, f_i\, f_c\, L$$

Where: R is the average rate of star formation; f is the fraction of stars with planetary systems; np is the number of planets per system suitable for the evolution of life; fi is the fraction of planets with intelligent life; fc is the fraction with civilizations; L is the average lifetime of such civilizations.

Scientific discoveries of the past two decades have shown that the number of such civilizations is immense. Conservative estimates range in the order of one million such civilizations in our own Milky Way Galaxy alone. (14)

If such ideas are correct, it seems reasonable to speculate that at least some of these civilizations have on occasion already visited our planet earth. Depending on what basis the calculations are done, cosmologists estimate the universe to be anywhere from 12 to 22 billion years old, give or take a couple of years. Yet our sun and solar system is believed to be no more than 5 billion years old. It is not at all impossible that there may have been civilizations as advanced as is ours today, long before our sun was even created. While many astronomers and scientists believe intelligent life does in fact exist elsewhere in the universe, many find it difficult to accept the fact it may have visited earth in the past or in the present. In part the arguments put forth against the idea of extraterrestrial contact are based on our present understanding of space/time, and the technologies we now have or can think of to bridge the cosmic distances needed to reach even the closest star system. These limitations may in fact exist in the real world. But the history of man is marked by supposedly insurmountable barriers which were overcome;

and some scientists, as well as science speculators, believe this is one of those temporary barriers in our own development.

METHOD

While it is one thing to believe that life probably exists elsewhere in the universe, and that at least some UFO reports represent potential new scientific information, it is quite another thing to connect the two. I believe both that life exists elsewhere (and some of it much more advanced intellectually and scientifically than on earth), and that the UFO phenomenon is a real one. But the view that some UFO reports are generated by space visitors is a hypothesis to be tested. I suspect that some UFO reports are in fact generated by someone else's space ships. But I also suspect that far fewer than 1 per cent of even the "legitimate" UFO reports are created from this source. The vast majority of such reports are more likely generated by natural events going on, be they solar plasmas not yet recognized as such or the migration of budworms. In particular, I doubt if any of the critter or occupant cases listed in this book are at all related to hypothetical space visitors. There are a couple that I hold back judgement on, but not many. In recent years many UFO investigators have concentrated much of their effort on the occupant reports since on face value these reports seem the shortest path to demonstrating that some UFOs are somebody else's space ships. Even though some of the occupant and critter cases may lead to new information about the real world, it is more likely that it will relate to dream states and altered states of consciousness (and the possible physical correlates of some of these states). Some of these cases even appear to include what is often referred to as extrasensory perception or knowledge, although I prefer to label it as a different mode of perception. If these conclusions prove to be true, then other kinds of UFO reports should be examined by those who are looking for the extraterrestrial connection.

The present state of the art of UFO research is largely at a proto-science level – not much more than the motley collection of largely anecdotal accounts. While this is due in part to the lack of public funding, it also reflects the fact that UFO research (at least that part done by investigators who believe there is in fact wheat in the chaff) has until recently been done almost entirely by amateurs with limited scientific and organizational training.

In my own study of occupant cases, I've arbitrarily divided the 90 cases in this catalogue into 9 categories, running from those with insufficient information to classify to those cases where the occupants allegedly physically interacted with the percipients. The categories run a spectrum from little involvement with the witnesses (fly-bys) to intense involvement (molesters). While the categories are arbitrary (and sometimes my labeling a particular case is arbitrary as well) some of them do in fact suggest that different kinds of events are generating these categories of occupant reports. There may be other more fruitful ways of dividing the cases, and one option is suggested in the concluding chapter. (15)

One of the difficulties of UFO research is that the definition of a UFO is so broad that at one level all of human knowledge can be subsumed under UFO research. Obviously, this is impractical as well as being scientifically unsound. I've elected to exclude some episodes that other researchers might justifiably argue should have been included in this work. Particularly obvious by its exclusion are the contactee cases, where the percipients allege that not only were they in physical contact with extraterrestrials, but that they received messages or warnings (often "telepathically") of one sort or another to convey to earth. In fact, some of the cases listed in the catalogue share features of the contactee experience. But rather than treat these kinds of cases superficially, I've elected to discuss them in another work. My own view, however, is that there is no reason to accept rubbish merely because it is alleged to have come from the mouth of a Venusian or Space Commander for this quadrant of the universe. Silly ideas are silly ideas no matter where they come from.

Although some of the characters listed in the catalogue would be included in anyone's list of "critters," I've omitted reference to non-"humanoid" kinds of critters (as well as to Sasquatch). This doesn't mean they haven't been reported. For instance, the April 6th, 1892, edition of the Calgary (Alberta) Tribune printed the following tale:

INDIAN MIRACLES

"...while a party of hunters were traveling they suddenly heard a great noise like thunder, and on looking up they saw two gigantic birds. One of the birds picked up one of the hunter's horses and flew away with it. While the other bird was attempting to take another horse one of the hunters shot it.

"The color of the bird that was killed was sky blue; the other was white. The tail of the bird that was killed was measured at three feet, and its wing from shoulder to tip was seven feet."

Unidentified flapping objects, like unidentified flying objects, have been around for a long time. I've even come across some instances where people swear they saw a monkey looking furry thing flying in the air. But the reports lack detail, and do not include any reference to a light source or UFO, so I've excluded them.

I do have one non-humanoid case that involves a UFO. In this case a man reported to me that he was near Beaver Lake, Alberta, on August 6th, 1972, when he felt compelled to go to a campsite where he was convinced he would see a UFO. He and two other men went that evening to the site and waited for several hours. It was now dark, and they had given up their UFO watch, when the three of them saw a light travel across the lake and pass behind some trees. Shortly afterwards, they heard the heavy footsteps of something breaking trail in the shrub and trees. They became scared, and fled to the car. As they drove along the highway, they could see giant tentacles and the octopus-like form of a creature that seemed to be trying to get in at them. They banged on the roof, but the creature remained. At one point they got out of the car and struggled with the octopus. They got back into the car, and by the time they reached Tofield, Alberta, their hitch hiking friend had disappeared. But this book will only discuss those humanoid looking entities which either are observed in, on or near a UFO, or else have been associated with the UFO corpus by having been discussed in a UFO book. A number of these latter cases seem to have no obvious connection with the UFO phenomenon.

Notes to Part 1

1. Herbert Joseph Strentz, A Survey of Press Coverage of Unidentified Flying Objects, 1947-1966, Ph.D thesis, Department of Journalism, Northwestern University, 1970

2. Edward U. Condon, Scientific Director, Final Report of the Scientific Study of Unidentified Flying Objects, 1968, p. 9. A number of criticisms of this report have been made by members of the scientific community. See, for instance: P.A. Sturrock, Evaluation of the Condon Report on the Colorado UFO Project, Stanford University Institute for Plasma Research, Report No. 599, October 1974

3. J. Allen Hynek, The UFO Experience: A Scientific Inquiry, 1972, p. 10.

4. In connection with this, a very useful guide to the many natural things going on in the world that can give rise to UFO reports is: Peter M. Millman, "Seven Maxims of UFOs-A Scientific Approach," Royal Astronomical Society of Canada Journal, Vol. 69, 1975, pp. 1175-188.

5. Edward U. Condon, op. cit., p. 2.

6. There is still some dispute as to whether there really is a phenomenon of ball lightning. A recent short summary is: Bruce H. Bailey, "Ball Lightning," Weatherwise, June 1977, pp. 99-105.

7. Philip J. Klass, UFOs Explained, 1974

8. Michael A. Persinger, "Transient Geophysical Bases for Ostensible UFO-Related Phenomena and Associated Verbal Behavior?" Perceptual and Motor Skills, Vol. A3, 1976, pp. 215-221; Yutaka Yasui, "A Summary of Studies on Luminous Phenomena Accompanied with Earthquakes," Dokkyo Medical University, 1974.

9. Philip S. Callahan, and R.W. Mankin, "Insects as unidentified flying objects," Applied Optics, November 1 1978, pp. 3355-3360.

10. Allen G. Mc Namara, "UFO's. What Are They?" Journal of the Canadian Air Traffic Control Association, Vol. 8, No. 1, 1976, pp. 10-12. Interestingly, there

are no references to psychology, philosophy or sociology studies in what is in large part a paper on the nature of belief and human understanding.

11. David Michael Jacobs, The UFO Controversy in America, Chapter 9. The Condon Committee and Its Aftermath, 1975

12. One way would be to develop curricula that encourage a critical and scientific approach to the UFO phenomenon. One suggestion for this is outlined in: Everett Richard Walter, The Study of Unidentified Flying Objects and its Adoption Within the Community College Curriculum, Ph.D thesis, Department of Education, Nova University, 1977

13. Steven J. Dick, Plurality of Worlds and Natural Philosophy: An Historical Study of the Origins of Belief in Other Worlds and Extraterrestrial Life, Ph.D thesis, Department of History and Philosophy of Science, Indiana University, 1977

14. Although now a decade old, perhaps the best popular book on the existence of life elsewhere is still: I.S. Shklovskii, and Carl Sagan, Intelligent Life in the Universe, 1966 The Journal of the British Interplanetary Society devotes many of its articles to the factors involved in interactions between our civilization and hypothetical interstellar cultures.

15. Ted Bloecher and David Webb have suggested a slightly different UFO-entity classification scheme. Ted Bloecher, "A Catalogue of Humanoid Reports for 1974," in MUFON 1975 UFO Symposium Proceedings, pp. 51-77; David Webb, 1973-Year of the Humanoids , 2nd edition, May 1976 When the promised humanoid catalogue being prepared by Bloecher and Webb is printed, it might be useful to see if the patterns proposed in this work hold true on a world scale.

UNKNOWNS AND THOSE INSIDE THE CRAFT

Type O: Insufficient Information

12 September 1950-Harmon Air Force Base, Newfoundland

20 September 1963-Saskatoon, Saskatchewan

14 August 1967-St. Charles, New Brunswick

September 1967-Langley, British Columbia

21 September 1968-Coaticook, Quebec

28 September 1968-Asbestos, Quebec

18 November 1973-Tracey, Quebec

17 February 1978-Dollard-des-Ormeaux, Quebec

As the name suggests, case histories in this category are impossible in most instances to classify. In most instances this is because of insufficient information; often the reference is no more than a potential lead which would lead to a much less spectacular case if tracked down. On more than one occasion, I've discovered that what had been reported to me as a spectacular occupant sighting with physical traces, multiple witnesses, etc., upon investigation turned out to be no more than a bright light hovering over a field at night.

In a few cases I've elected to place the episode in this limbo category as I've found the potential connection with the supposed UFO extremely tenuous, and the object observed not to be particularly unusual in itself. Obviously, other investigators (particularly those who have passed them on) feel otherwise.

Such, in my opinion, is the widely (at least in French language publications) publicized incident which occurred on the road between Tracey and Montreal, Quebec, on November 18th, 1973 (1)

That Sunday evening four young women were in a car driving southwest from Tracey on highway 3 towards Montreal. Shortly out of Tracey, they noticed a luminous ball in front of them alongside the highway. Just after they passed by it, the white ball began to move, pacing the car alongside the St. Lawrence River. The light paced them all the way to the suburbs of Montreal.

Before reaching Contrecoeur, their car, as well as the many other vehicles on the road, had to enter and pass through a kind of pink cloud hanging over the roadway. Just after they left the cloud they noticed a "small man" standing exactly on the white dividing line of the road. He appeared to be sweeping the road with a large brush, and seemed unaware of the traffic passing close by. Further up the road two or three persons, dressed in black, were standing near the road close to a vehicle in the ditch.

Some investigators believe this to be a genuine UFO occupant case – that something extraordinary took place that evening. (2) In part, this conclusion was made because of the fact that a lone entity was observed on the roadway, and the assumption was made that public works employees only work in visible teams. On many occasions I've come across a lone workman shoveling or sweeping on the remote highways of Alberta (their fellow workers being some miles down the road or on the other side of a hill), so I don't find this kind of logic very convincing. So I've elected to put this into the limbo category pending more information than has been given in print.

Type 1: Fly-Bys

Autumn 1796 -New Mines, Nova Scotia

June 1954-Harptree, Saskatchewan

Autumn 1954 or 1955-Calgary, Alberta

31 May 1962-Montreal, Quebec

July 1967-St-Stanislas-de-Kotska, Quebec

Mid-August 1967-Welland, Ontario

November 1968-North of Yellowknife, N.W.T.

1969-Calgary, Alberta

13 October 1969-Vancouver, British Columbia

29 July 1973-Ottawa, Ontario

4 February 1978-Scarborough, Ontario

The briefest, simplest kind of occupant case for which there is enough information to make a classification involves one or more UFOs perceived as flying past. The UFO is usually described as having some detail, particularly "port-holes" through which shadows or silhouettes are visible. These shadows are interpreted either by the witness or by the investigator as occupants controlling the flight of their craft

Perhaps the earliest documented occupant case in North America took place in the autumn of 1796 near the Bay of Fundy, Nova Scotia. (3) The incident was recorded in the diary of Simeon Perkins, an historical figure in those parts. According to his account, 15 ships were observed flying to the east about sunrise by a young girl and two men. In one of the ships they could see a man forward with his hand outstretched. The ships were so near the three that they could make out the sides and ports of the flying boats.

Most fly-bys are less exotic and detailed, involving no more than a shadow seen through a porthole. Such is the case about 2:30 A.M., in November 1968 when three men – pilot, co-pilot, and flight engineer – were at 10,000 feet in a Bristol 170 approximately 150 miles north of Yellowknife, N.W.T. (4) For about five minutes they observed a disk which approached their plane and came as close as 1,000 feet away. For part of the time they could see about a dozen windows along the side, and through one of the center windows they spotted what appeared to be a humanlike form. The UFO paced them for a while, and then disappeared almost instantly.

Type 2: Stopping for the View

1 July 1969-Olds, Alberta

1 January 1970-Cowichan, British Columbia

July 1975-Radium Hot Springs, British Columbia

November 1975 Montreal, Quebec

This category is very similar to fly-bys, and would in fact be classified the same in many category schemes. In these cases, the UFO and its associated occupants appear to have stopped for the view, often very close to the witness (no multiple witness cases here – at least not for the occupant), and often, it would appear, on "purpose."

A widely publicized sighting of this type took place on New Year's Day 1970 around 5 A.M. at the Cowichen District Hospital, Duncan, British Columbia. (5) Mrs. Doreen Kendall, a registered nurse, opened up the drapes to one of the wards and observed a circular craft with a transparent dome. The craft was no more than 40 feet outside the window, and she could see two figures inside the dome – one at an instrument panel, the other standing beside him. They were described as being more than six feet tall, with "nice" physiques, and hands that looked human. They were dressed in dark clothing similar to that worn by pilots.

While Mrs. Kendall stood watching, one of the entities turned and appeared to look directly at her. He then put his hand on the back of the other occupant who was sitting down. The entity seated then pulled back on what appeared to be a joy stick, and the UFO tilted sideways and began to fly off. Only then did she think to summon other witnesses, who only arrived in time to see the craft moving off.

Notes to Part 2

1. Claude MacDuff, Le Proces des Soucoupes Volantes, 1975 pp. 173-180; Marc Leduc, "Les Observations du 18.\1.73," ufo-Quebec, Ne. 3, 1975, pp. 4-6.

2. A recent article has drawn attention to some similarities between this case and two others; one at Brabant, Belgium in mid-December 1973 the other at Uden, The Netherlands in autumn 1973 Christiane Piens, "A Propos de: Trois

Humanoides et Une Brosse Aspirateur," UFO INFO, No. Sh, Decembre 1978 pp. 4-6.

3. Various US and Canadian newspapers.

4. Jeff Holt, "Rencontre avec un UFO," UFO-Quebec, No. 4, 1975 p. 17

5. Letters in APRO files. See also: Coral Lorenzen and Jim Lorenzen, Encounters with UFO Occupants, 1976, pp. 391-392; John Magor, Our UFO Visitors, 1977 pp. 217-219.

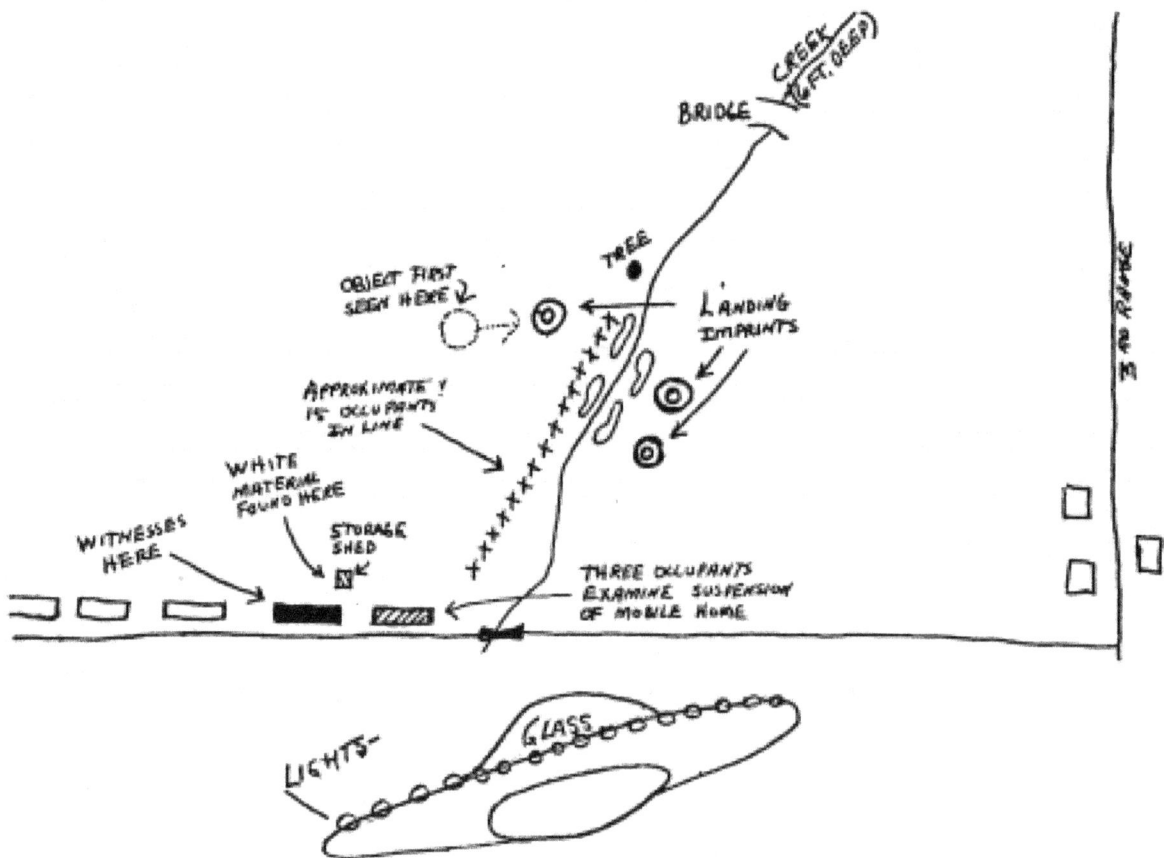

The pilot manipulated what appeared to be a "joy stick" and the disk tilted sharply and disappeared instantly.

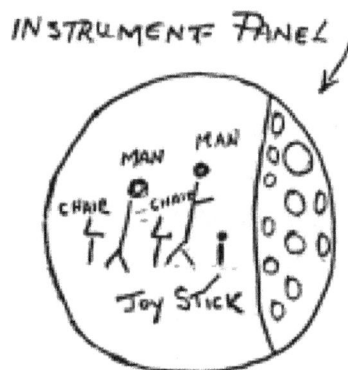

Drawn by Witness

PROJECT MAGNET

STROLLERS AND OTHERS OUT ON THE TOWN

Type 3: Strollers (no UFO)

October 1932-Joliette, Quebec

Winter 1955-Ste-Therese, Quebec

26 July 1968-Riviere-du-Loup, Quebec

4 August 1968-Montreal, Quebec

6 August 1968-Ste-Gertrude, Quebec

14 September 1968-Drummondville, Quebec

15 September 1968-Drummondville, Quebec

12 July 1971-Notre-Dame-du-Nord, Quebec

31 December 1973-East of Medicine Hat, Alberta

9 October 1975-North Bay, Ontario

The entities in this category are a motley bunch of characters, and might better be placed among the many ghost and fairy tales. In all of these cases, quite unusual entities of one sort or another have been observed, and somehow a connection is made (not always by the investigator or the witness) between these critters and the UFO phenomenon. About all that ties these cases is their strangeness.

My favorite case is one collected by Bill Holt of the Edmonton UFO Society, and is one that might even warrant a step up to category A. Bill interviewed a man who had been driving east of Medicine Hat, Alberta, on Highway 1 on his way back home in Brooks, Alberta. It was New Year's Eve 1973 and about 10:30 P.M. He noticed a very bright light in the rearview mirror. At first he thought it must be the lights from an oncoming train, but then he realized that there are no tracks along that section of highway. Soon afterwards he spotted an 8-feet-tall man running in the ditch alongside the highway. The truck was hitting at least 60 mph at the time, yet the critter not only kept pace, but came up to the truck and placed its hands on the roof and hood before disappearing. The man swore he hadn't been drinking, though he had been on the road for some time, and fatigue may very well have contributed to his kind of experience.

> Type 4: Strollers (UFO)
> Winter 1924-Saskatchewan
> 12 June 1929-Fermeneuve, Quebec
> 1948-Svastika, Ontario
> 2 July 1954-Garson, Ontario
> 7 August 1954-Hemingford, Ontario
> 19 September 1963-Saskatoon, Saskatchewan
> Late 1960s-Didsbury, Alberta
> End July 1965-Trois-Rivieres, Quebec
> Early April 1966 -Calgary, Alberta
> 4 April 1966-Trenton, Ontario
> 12 August 1967-Richibucto, New Brunswick
> 30 October 1967-Melfort, Saskatchewan
> 28 July 1968-St. Stanislas-de-Kotska, Quebec
> 29 Aug.-1 Sept. 1968-Coleraine, Quebec
> 26 April 1969-Calgary, Alberta
> 11 July 1970-Trois-Rivieres, Quebec
> 28 November 1972-Sarre, Quebec
> 25 June 1974-Drummondville, Quebec
> 7 October 1975-Bracebridge, Ontario
> 6 August 1976-Gaspesie, Quebec
> 6 January 1977-Montreal, Quebec
> 6 April 1977-Ste-Dorothee, Quebec

Although the 22 cases in this category vary widely in the descriptions of the physical characteristics of the entities and their associated craft, all involve some sort of entity observed either to actually emerge from or enter into a UFO, or else an object was sighted in close proximity to an entity. Many of these cases are multiple-witness ones. Such was true on the night of June 25th, 1979, near Drummondville, Quebec. (1)

That night a young man was watching television about 1:15 A.M. when he heard a strange bum...bum...bum kind of noise outside his mobile home. He lifted the living room curtain and saw a reddish orange object hovering in a field to the northeast. The object was so bright, it almost hurt his eyes to stare at it

He went to the bedroom and woke up his wife and the two of them could

114

now hear a buzzing sound outside the window. When they looked out they saw a 6-feet-tall entity no more than 15 feet from the trailer. It appeared to be metallic and moved stiffly. Glowing red horizontal bars could be seen where a torso should be. The entity moved and acted like a robot, first inspecting the interior of a pre-fab storage shed near their trailer. The couple soon noticed three more similar entities examine a nearby mobile home. The trailer park had just opened up and their trailer was the only one occupied; the nearby trailer had yet to be placed on its foundation. The two of them watched the activities of these robots for the next three hours. At one time as many as 15 entities could be seen together in one line close to a nearby creek in the direction of the UFO. Later on three landing traces were discovered; rings about 17 feet in diameter as well as imprints which appeared to be caused by legs from the UFOs. The grass appeared to have suffered no damage from heat.

A quite different kind of entity was observed by Robert Suffern around 9 P.M., on October 7th, 1975, near his farm at Bracebridge, Ontario. (2) He was at home when his sister phoned and asked if he could see an orange glow in the sky. She was concerned that the barn might be on fire. When Mr. Suffern drove out onto the farm to investigate, his headlights shone on a landed object in the middle of the road. It appeared to be 12-14 feet in diameter, and approximately 8-9 feet high. Its surface was silver colored, and appeared to have no details. When the headlights hit the object, it shot straight up and out of sight. Mr. Suffern then turned the car round and headed back for the farmhouse. About 400 yards down the road, he slammed on the brakes to avoid hitting a strange critter on the road. The entity was no more than 10 or 15 feet away and seemed no more than 4 or 5 feet tall. It seemed out of proportion, with legs that were short and an upper body too big for the head. It walked like a "midget," awkward and yet easily. As Mr. Suffern passed by, the entity spun round and headed back in the direction he seemed to be coming from —a field on the same side of the road as where the UFO was just a few moments earlier. The entity grabbed a wire fence and leaped over as if weightless. It was dressed in silver coveralls. The entity could only be seen for a few seconds as it raced off, presumably wondering why its buddies on the craft had taken off without him.

Notes to Part 3

1. Wido Hoville, "'Robot' occupants reported," SKYLOOK, No. 8A, November 1974 pp. 10-11; Marc Leduc, "Un Atterrissage et des Humanoides a Drummondville," UFO-Quebec, No. 1, 1975 pp. 10-12; Claude MacDuff, Le Procesdes Soucoupes Volantes, 1975 pp. 197-204.

2. Report by Henry McKay to Center for UFO Studies, Evanston, Illinois; Canadian UFO Report, Vol. 3, No. 3, 1975 p. 5.

PROJECT MAGNET

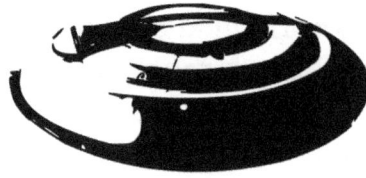

TOURISTS AND PIT STOPS

Type 5: Tourists
1948 Svastika, Ontario
3 October 1954, Lac la Pause, Quebec
1960s, northern Manitoba
13 June 1967, Caledonia, Ontario
28 July 1968, Upton, Quebec
14 September 1969, Beauharnois, Quebec
9 June 1971, Rosedale, Alberta

The tourists or vacationers appear to be amateur zoologists and geologists. They don't appear to be the equivalent of astronauts or cosmonauts; but we may be making a mistake if we assume all hypothetical space visitors must be extra-terrestrial scientists. In these cases, it's almost as if the entities were flying by and noticed a nice rock formation to take back to Aunt Martha, and landed for a moment to take home a few souvenirs. If this is true, one must ask why they landed so close to a witness when in most instances it would have been easy to avoid human contact. It may not be insignificant that most of these cases involve UFOs that left physical traces.

One of the better documented of these cases occurred near Rosedale, Alberta, on June 9th, 1971. (1) Esther A. Clappison was attracted to a light shining through the window. It was just before 9 P.M., and a full moon was out, yet this light still was brilliant through the window. She went outside with her dog to investigate the source of the light, and spotted a rectangular object on the ground about 200 feet from the house. Two entities were inside and could be seen through a transparent wall. A third entity was outside, apparently collecting rocks. All were dressed in olive green costumes which covered all of their bodies.

As soon as she noticed the entities inside the craft, they seemed to be trying to attract the attention of their buddy outside. Ms. Clappison wanted to get closer, but her dog was pulling at its leash, trying to run into the house. She followed, and hoped to summon her brother who was inside the house. But when she got inside and looked out, the UFO and its three entities could no longer be seen. Next morning a burned area just over 20 feet in length was discovered near where the object was spotted.

Type 6: Pit Stops
August 1914-Georgia Bay, Ontario
Summer 1935-Nipawin, Saskatchewan
2 July 1950-Sawbill Bay, Ontario
Late July 1950-Sawbill Bay, Ontario
August 1965-Ottawa, Ontario
15 August 1967-Port Perry, Ontario
23 August 1967-Joyceville, Ontario
June 1969-Overton, Nova Scotia
6 October 1973-St-Mathias, Quebec
April 1974-Timmins, Ontario
14 October 1975-Peers, Alberta

Pit stops appear to involve serious business, at least from the standpoint of the hypothetical occupants. In these cases the entities appear to be either repairing their craft or replenishing supplies, usually water. These kinds of occupant cases are perhaps the most consistent with many of our preconceived notions about what space travelers might do on a planet they don't want to establish social contact with, yet have some pressing business to do on. Some of the best known Canadian cases come from this category.

These cases almost always involve more than one short stature occupant and always involve a large craft with structural detail, often detected near water (lake or slew or ocean), and often physical traces are associated with their presence.

Perhaps the best documented case of this kind was the sighting of June 26-27, 1959, in Boainai, Papua, New Guinea. (2) Thirty-eight witnesses, including Reverend William Gill, an Anglican priest and head of the mission in Boainai, observed up to four entities on the superstructure of a disk shaped object which hovered above the village. At one point, when the natives waved at the four forms on the deck, they appeared to wave back. However, much of the time they appeared to be manipulating something on the deck. A blue light, like a spotlight, emanated skyward from time to time from the center of the craft. The object appeared over the village for two successive nights, although this sighting was just one of many on the island that year.

PROJECT MAGNET

A case almost as well publicized, though less well documented, is alleged to have taken place in August 1914 near Georgia Bay, Ontario. (3) As documented in footnotes 10 and 11 of the UFO occupant and critter catalogue, this episode may very well be cooked up and based in fact on the alleged encounter of 2 July 1950 which itself is likely a fabrication. According to William Kiehl, he along with two other Americans and a Canadian family were camped near the water. Late in the afternoon one of the family's children noticed a deer at the water's edge, and the deer's gaze drew her attention to an unusual craft hovering above the water about 150 feet from shore. Everyone observed the object, which was shaped like a slightly flattened hemisphere. Two entities could be seen on the superstructure which surrounded the craft. These critters appeared to be no more than 4 feet tall, and were clad in tight-fitting iridescent suits. They were dressed in greenish-purple suits, and were manipulating a green hose which dangled above the water. This hose appeared to be controlled by some mechanism at the top of the craft

After a few moments, three other small entities appeared at the upper part of the craft, but they were dressed in khaki colored suits. They also wore box-shaped yellow headpieces. These three seemed to be busy working on three pipes which protruded from the top of the craft. They then disappeared, and the craft rose suddenly from the water as if they had been frightened by something.

One of the occupants was still outside, clinging onto a chrome colored ring around the superstructure. The craft flew out of sight with the critter still hanging on. Like his distant cousin in Bracebridge, Ontario, his buddies seemed in a hurry to leave with or without him.

There are a number of inconsistencies and loose ends in this case. In addition to looking like a carbon copy of the July 1950 incident at Sawbill Bay, Ontario, the dimensions written by Kiehl in his letters, and the drawings he made to illustrate the event don't always match. For instance, if the craft was in fact thought to be 9 or 12 feet wide, the entities as drawn above couldn't have been 4 feet Cases like this one could be classic ones, and major steps towards proving that at least some UFO sightings are in fact someone else's space craft But not this one.

Notes to Part 4

1. W. K. Allan, "Humanoids and craft seen at Rosedale," Flying Saucer Review. Case Histories, No. 10, June 1972 pp. 4-5; Brian James, "The Rosedale Humanoids: Further Details," Flying Saucer Review. Case Histories, No. 16 August 1973, pp. 6-7.

2. Norman E.G. Cruttwell, "Flying Saucers Over Papua," Flying Saucer Review. Special Issue No. 4, August 1971, pp. 3-38.

3. Letters to APRO and Timothy Green Beckley; Coral and Jim Lorenzen, Flying Saucer Occupants, 1967 pp. 19-23.

PEEPING TOMS AND MOLESTERS

Type 7: Peeping Toms

Mid-August 1958-Bells Corner, Ontario

August 1961-Wetaskiwin, Alberta

July 1965-Rosemont, Quebec

Spring 1966-Wetaskiwin, Alberta

Early Summer 1966-Qualicum Beach, British Columbia

Early 1970-Brandon, Manitoba

4 November 1972-Clyde, Alberta

22 November 1973-Joliette, Quebec

29 July 1976-Sabrevois, Quebec

Some of the events subsumed under the first six categories may prove to be real physical encounters with extraterrestrial entities. My view is that the jury is still out on those few cases which warrant such consideration. However, the peeping toms and molesters don't convince me, even though there may be physical components to these episodes, which in principle are measurable. From this perspective, it's unfortunate that much of the current interest in, and alleged proof of, the exo-terran origin of occupant cases has been based on a few classic cases from these last two categories.

Peeping toms or voyeurs almost always are reported by a couple or small group of close friends (the only Canadian exceptions to this rule I've investigated involve people who before and after the entity episode had "psychic" episodes which included visual images). Normally, one or more is awakened from sleep in the middle of the night, or from a nap, or else is doing a dull routine task such as washing dishes. Upon awakening, they discover one or more critters close by, often in the same room or peering through a window. In most cases the percipients would pass it off as a simple dream state. And I would as well if it wasn't for the fact that in many of these cases there are independent witnesses who claim at the same time to have witnessed a UFO hovering quite close to the place where the entity was spotted. Perhaps it is significant that the UFO is never described as having detail such as portholes or superstructure, but always as a bright white or blue light. The following case from Wetaskiwin is typical. (1)

About 3:30 A.M. on August 5th, 1961, a couple was awakened to discover two figures standing near their bed. They both attempted to get up, but felt paralyzed. And both felt unusually content and at peace as the two male figures spoke first to each other, and then to the husband (male chauvinists, or speaking to the dominant of the couple?). The entities were small, perhaps 4 or 5 feet tall at the most. They were smartly dressed in a two-piece suit of soft, dark colored cloth-like material with belts around the middle. Each wore a face helmet or glass bubble behind his head. Neither walked, but floated through the air. The entities spoke with the man for what seemed a minute, and suggested to him that they would come back and see him again. All at once, one of the entities said to the other, "I think they're waking up on us. We'd better go." With that, the two figures disappeared instantly in front of the couple with a noise like wind blowing through a pipe. As soon as they disappeared, the couple could again move. The husband rushed out the back of the house, but he discovered nothing out of the ordinary.

Ordinarily it would seem only wise to regard a case like this as no more (and no less) than an interesting dream shared by the two. The symbols might have meaning for the two, but are of limited public interest. But in this episode, as well as in others, there was another witness. Unknown to the couple, their neighbor to the east was awake at the same time, and observed a bluish brilliant globe in front of their house at the same time they observed the two entities. The globe was estimated to be 25 feet in diameter, and slowly lifted off the ground, before gradually accelerating to the north.

And it is not a unique case. Other voyeur and peeping tom episodes have taken place the same time independent witnesses are spotting a light. Such appears to have happened in Joliette, Quebec, around 2 A.M. November 22nd, 1973. (2) In this case, a woman felt restless and couldn't sleep. When she got up and walked to the kitchen she observed a 4 feet tall "thing" with a round head and two very bright eyes glowing with a phosphorescence staring at her through the window. Around the head or helmet there was a bright halo. She observed the entity with unusual peace and calm for about 15 seconds before it disappeared in front of her. Only then did she realize that something strange had happened, and she went to waken her husband in the next room. When he looked outside he could find nothing unusual except for a dog that was scared to death. There were quite a few reports of strange lights made that morning in that part of Joliette.

In these kinds of episodes, location in physical space is critical. The place one is in determines how one perceives the event. Whether the episode is precipitated by mental processes in the group experiencing the event, or else by a physical distortion of the environment, remains to be rigorously demonstrated. But the physical location in space is important in understanding what is behind these kinds of experiences. The alteration in perception is associated with some change in the environment that can be observed as a blue or white light source if observed at a far enough distance. Whether the change in the environment generated the episode, or the mental episode generated the change in the environment, is yet to be tested, but these cases suggest the correlation of the two.

Both an active and passive percipient are often involved in such cases. That is, while voyeur and peeping tom episodes may only involve one person who reported seeing an entity (although many of the cases are multiple witness), it seems that there is always another person close by, often asleep as well, and always either a spouse or close relative, or someone emotionally very close. In those few exceptions I know, the person reports a history of "psychic" episodes normally with a highly visual content. In those cases which involve at least a couple, it may be that one uses the other as a mental catalyst as it were, or else that they are working something out together. All of the cases in Canada that involve more than a single person in fact are two adults of the opposite sex which I doubt is an accidental pairing. The one exception is an adult man and his mother. These cases are highly personal, and the psychological makeup and history of the percipients is critical to understanding what is going on. This doesn't rule out the physical components that the cases suggest is there, but it does suggest that what communication occurs is with the witnesses' projections rather than with hypothetical extraterrestrials.

While being an intensely mental and psychological experience, perhaps involving involuntary psychic activities, such episodes seem to have at least one fundamental physical attribute which has already been mentioned. Those close to the focus experience a benign entity, often described in religious dimensions, who may or may not actually converse with them. Those further away perceive a bright light with no structural detail. In these cases, as well as in the classic one at Fatima, Portugal in 1917 (3), it may not be that the principal witnesses were "selected" as is often assumed or asserted, but that they were at the right spot at the right time to be affected by some physical change in the environment. My bias is that if you or I had walked beside the young girl at Fatima, for instance, we would have either shared her vision, or else hatched our own.

Wilbert Smith and Jack Buchanan have documented an episode which took place the week of August 18th, 1958, which suggests that on at least one occasion a person actually entered and left the physical location where perception seems to have been altered. (4) The principal witness may have been mapping the psychological space around the event. This episode took place in a rural center about 5 miles west of Ottawa, Ontario. About 10:45 in the evening, Mrs. Couturier glanced out of her window and noticed a patch of bluish light about 25 feet south of the house. She called to her son, and the two of them went outside to investigate further. Although Mrs. Couturier was brave and walked up to within a couple of feet of the light, her son was anxious and stayed further away, urging extreme caution. He only observed the bright blue light the whole time. However, when Mrs. Couturier walked right up to the light, she observed what appeared to be a small person lying face down on the ground with its face lifted so its eyes were visible, but not the lower part of the face. The light seemed to be radiating from the entities' eyes (as was true in the case at Joliette, Quebec, and Clyde, Alberta). She felt calm and peaceful as she watched for about a minute before the pleading of her son convinced her to return into the house.

Type 8: Molesters

1912, western Canada

1960s, Lac St-Jean, Quebec

Autumn 1966, Island Lake, Manitoba

17 November 1967, Calgary, Alberta

Late July 1968, St. Bruno, Quebec

Summer 1969, Trois-Rivieres, Quebec

End February 1970, Terrace, British Columbia

29 October 1973, Toronto, Ontario

The molesters or abductors complete our mapping of occupant and critter sightings in Canada. Although all of these reports involve some kind of physical contact with the entities, many of these cases share characteristics with the previous category of voyeurs and peeping toms. The cases in Canada can, for convenience at least, be divided into two subgroups. In one, young children are given "candies" or other goodies to entice them to visit the craft of strange "dwarf-like" beings. Such a case was reported from northern Manitoba autumn 1966. (5) In the other subgroup, the percipients (usually young boys, in the Canadian cases at least), by one coercive means or another, are put through "physical" examinations either outside or inside the craft. These kinds of abductions in past years were largely ignored. But recently they have received a great deal of attention. Feature movies, books and articles have been presented about a few classic cases of abduction – and all of these have presented the story with an extraterrestrial connection.

The classic abduction case happened when Betty and Barney Hill were driving home to Portsmouth, New Hampshire, from Montreal, Quebec, on the night of September 19th, 1961. (6) They both remembered sighting a UFO when they arrived home, and noticed markings on their car and that their cloths were dirty and messed up. But it was only after subsequent nightmares and clinical hypnotic regressions that the abduction experience became conscious. They remembered that intelligent entities had forced them aboard the UFO and performed physical examinations on the two of them. In addition, Betty later recalled viewing a star map, which she later reproduced and which has been the subject of much controversy over whether or not it actually reproduces the stars as they appear from a nearby star system. Obviously, if this and similar cases represent real physical abductions, they are not only proof that intelligent life exists elsewhere and visits earth from time to time, but they also are potential sources of information about advanced sciences and technologies.

As interesting as this possibility is, I doubt that this case is much different from the peeping tom and voyeur cases. While it likely involves a mental projection created by the two that would have been impossible for either Betty or Barney to have created alone, that is quite a different phenomenon than a physical abduction by aliens.

The most publicized Canadian case which involved molesters or abductors is a UFO sighting which was quite frightening at the time, but which seemed only to be a UFO sighting until a subsequent dream. This was also true with Betty and Barney Hill. Around 5:45 P.M., November 17th, 1967, a young man left the home of one of his school chums and began on what is normally a short walk home. (7) However, this evening he didn't arrive home until 6:30 when his older sister saw him dash in through the front door. She followed him upstairs, and found him trying to hide under the bed. He was in a state of shock, and told her that he'd been chased by a "flying saucer." One of his shoes was missing and was later discovered outside along the road.

His sister questioned him, and he said he'd been walking home across the field when he heard a humming noise. When he looked up he saw a large saucer shaped object with lights or portholes around it. The next thing he remembered was running home with the saucer still overhead.

In late April of the following year the young man had a nightmare, and afterwards was convinced that in fact he had been abducted and taken aboard the craft he witnessed back in November. Under hypnotic regression, he recalled being taken up into the saucer by an orange beam of light, being put on a table and wheeled through a room of instruments, and being undressed by critters who had "rough brown skin like a crocodile," and who wore no clothing. He remembered that the critters had holes for their ears and noses, and just sort of a slit where their mouths should be. Their eyes came out on a slant.

Notes to Part 5

1. John Brent Musgrave, "Cosmic Voyeurs—19th and 20th Century Style," Flying Saucer Review, Vol. 23, No. 2, 1977, PP. 26-27.

2. Wido Hoville, "Enquetes au Quebec: Joliette 1973 UFO-Quebec, No. 2, 1975 pp. 7-8.

3. Ray Stanford, Fatima Prophecy: Days of Darkness, Promise of Light, 1974 Jacques Vallee, The Invisible College, 1975

4. W. B. Smith, and J. R. Buchanan, "The Bells Corner Mystery," Topside, June 1960 pp. 3-4.5. Letter to NICAP.

6. John G. Fuller, The Interrupted Journey: Two Lost Hours "Aboard a Flying Saucer", 1966

7. W. K. Allan, "Crocodile-Skinned Entities at Calgary," Flying Saucer Review, vol. 20, No. 6, 1974, pp. 25-26.

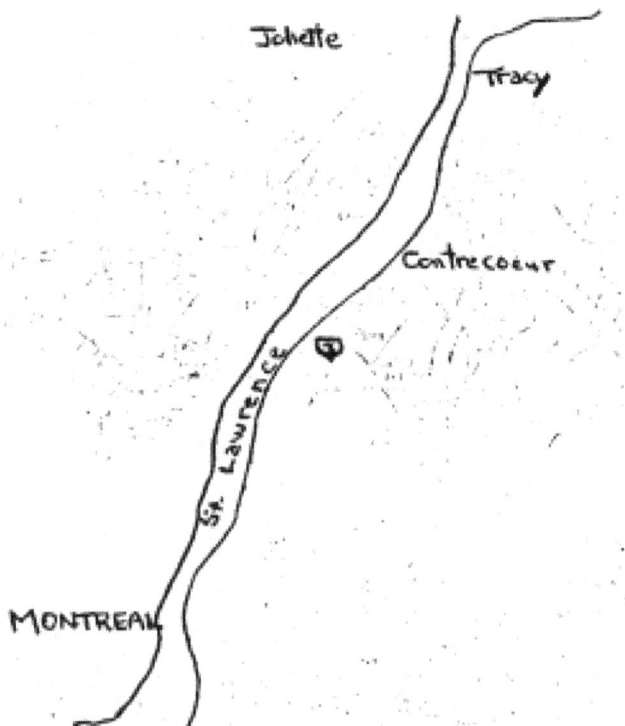

CONCLUSIONS

The quality of UFO reports depends on the individual investigator. There are no standards or guidelines to assess what a "genuine" UFO report is other than the very broad definitions suggested by Condon or Hynek. In addition, it should be kept in mind that in many instances the social status and public image of each investigator or person in a position to receive UFO reports often determines what kind of reports are likely to come his way. If the witness has observed a strange light in the sky, he's more likely to get in touch with a planetarium for possible astronomical identification, than he is if the object was a huge disc in the backyard out of which two dwarfs emerged, picked a rose off a bush, and then got back into their craft and took off. Normally, whatever else may be causing such an experience, the percipient knows it wasn't a misidentified planet or star, and there is little reason to phone a university or planetarium for an astronomical identification.

In short, the kind of UFO experience one has will in large part determine what community you will report it to or ask further information from. In general, I've found that the more strange the event the smaller the community one is likely to report the experience to. And UFO occupant cases are among the strangest and most difficult cases to learn about. While some UFO witnesses seek publicity, most in fact shun it. And it is not surprising that most of the occupant cases listed in the catalogue were collected by individual investigators rather than by official agencies such as National Research Council, police, etc. In fact, most of the cases have been collected by a handful of investigators, and one must keep this in mind when attempting to determine patterns in the sightings. Due to the present nature of collecting such reports, it is quite easy for the interests and prejudices of these few investigators to be hidden within the reports. There are as yet no controls on the collection of UFO reports.

Some of these cases may have an extraterrestrial connection. The jury may still be out on a handful of these cases. But looking through these reports I find little to suggest that very many could in any way have been generated by extraterrestrial visitors. There are those who like to argue that somehow the space visi-

125

tors would be so advanced that their actions would appear illogical or even magical to us. But even granted the obvious, that any civilization that has reached earth by this time may be very much in advance of us technologically, it doesn't follow that their actions will be beyond our comprehension. Unless one wants to believe the universe is one vast psycho ward, or that earth in particular is, then the notion that the motley gang of characters in this catalogue represents some of the universe's most intelligent specimens is just preposterous.

If there is an extraterrestrial connection to some UFO reports, then other kinds of reports are more likely candidates. It may be, for instance, that some of the "mother craft" sightings where one or more smaller objects emerge from or enter into a recognizable craft may in the end prove to be what on face value they suggest themselves to be – a scientific reconnaissance mission. Some of these sightings are multiple-independent-witness ones which include trained personnel. On face value, anyway, they would seem to be as likely candidates as the occupant cases. And anyone searching for the proposed connection between some UFOs and extraterrestrial life is not going to find a shortcut by concentrating on the occupant cases.

UFOs come in all shapes, sizes, colors, and display many different patterns of behavior. Some are noisy; others quiet. Some affect car radios when close by; others don't. Without having done a detailed, computer-based analysis on the data, it does appear that there are at least a few correlations between the description of the UFO and the description of the behavior of its occupants. All of the pit stop cases detail a highly mechanical looking UFO, often with portholes, superstructures and protruding pipes or aerials. If these cases, in fact, are mostly fabrications, then the source is obvious. If some of these cases, for example, the classic case in New Guinea in 1959 or the Saskatchewan case in 1935 turn out to be authentic cases, they seem to be some of the few occupant cases that in fact are generated by our proposed space visitors. In addition, pit stops are almost always reported to have taken place near a large body of water such as a lake, system of slews, or ocean. Presumably the occupants needed to take on the water. There also appears to be a correlation between voyeur or peeping tom cases (and many abduction or molester cases) and the report of a bright blue or white light which has no visible details.

There is enough evidence to strongly suggest such a correlation is real, yet I don't believe it has an extraterrestrial connection, but is some physical change on earth, be it a plasma or something else. While there may be some correlation between some kinds of occupant cases and the kinds of critters or entities, the correlation is more general, and not specific as to shoe size or color. Pit stops again appear to be consistent in describing smallish, suited fellows who appear in groups rather than as ones or twos; and abduction cases often make reference to the eyes – either how large they were or how bright they were, sometimes even giving off beams of light. Many of the UFO occupants seem to be unique, and it can be argued either are completely generated by the percipients' unconscious, or, to one degree or another, filled in by it. The motley collection of beasties, androids and ghosties that make up a large part of the UFO catalogue of entities is likely inhabited by such creatures.

I've elected to sort out these cases on the basis of the social or work activity in which the entities are reported to have been engaged (e.g., "repairing their craft," flying by, picking up rocks and grass, etc.). But there are other, and potentially more useful, ways to sort out entity cases. Greater attention might be spent on looking at the patterns in the witnesses themselves. Some of these patterns have already been mentioned. For instance, that voyeur or peeping tom cases always involve either a close couple or small group, or else an individual with a history of "psychic" episodes with highly visual content.

Many of the abduction or molester cases also share the same kind of constituency. The type of behavior the percipient was engaged in immediately prior to the encounter is another potentially useful way to sort out cases. Many, if not all, of the voyeur and abduction cases involve people who were either actually asleep, or else doing dull routine tasks such as driving long distances or washing dishes. These states of mind are likely key elements in setting off the encounter experience. Although I've not done a quantitative study, I also suspect that in those entity cases that appear to be largely subjective or have a large unconscious element in them, that patterns will emerge that are different for adolescence than for childhood or adulthood.

Amateurs have no business becoming part time clinicians, or hobby psychologists. But the fact remains that field investigators in particular should be more aware of the psychological, and potentially pathological, elements that come into play in some of the entity cases. (1) I know of one case in Alberta that appears to have been a contributing factor to a suicide. Relatives state the man was never the same after an occupant sighting; and although it is debatable whether the sighting actually triggered off a depression, or else was just one of many symptoms, it obviously should have been a sign to someone that some kind of counseling or adjustment needed to be made.

Many of these occupant encounters appear to be of the same stuff as dreams. In fact, some may be no more than dreams remembered as reality. However, even if this is true, some of the peeping tom and abduction cases appear to be cases where the dream is shared in some way. A number of investigators have speculated that the so-called ESP experience is more commonly found in the dreaming state than in the conscious state. Drs. Montague Ullman and Stanley Krippner at the Dream Laboratory of New York's Maimonides Medical Center Psychiatry Department in particular have experimented with dream telepathy. They have documented what they believe are genuine cases where the dreams of target people have been demonstrably altered by the physical acting out of certain messages or feelings of a "sender." For example, the sender might stand in a cold shower during a REM period of the target person who was asleep. When awakened, the dreamer would recount being caught in a cold rainstorm. If the witness testimony is reliable, many of the voyeur and some of the abduction cases appear to be very similar kinds of experiences. (Some have argued that this was the case with Betty and Barney Hill). Presumably, the submissive partner shared the dream of the dominant partner, though there is always the possibility that somehow they worked out the dream together.

In recent years a great amount of attention has been paid to the use of hypnotic time regressions in the investigation of UFO experiences, particularly abduction cases. (2) A number of abduction stories have been detailed, or actually discovered, by means of these techniques. It must always be kept in mind that such information is highly questionable, and Alvin Lawson has documented that imaginary abductees come up with stories that closely parallel the alleged "real" abductions. (3) However, even though many investigators have accepted this newfound tool, little attention has been drawn to the fact that many of these cases (and again particularly, but not exclusively, the voyeurs and abductions) are quite likely generated by hypnotic trance states in the first place. Many of the features considered as signs of the induction of hypnotic trance are just those features described by the UFO entity percipient. (4) For instance, just as a patient in hypnotic trance often remains immobile, almost always the percipient reports that he felt paralyzed and couldn't budge. If hypnotic trance is, as some clinicians maintain, an active process wherein the unconscious is active, but not directed by the conscious mind, then the entities reported in a great number of these cases have likely been brought up from the unconscious. It seems likely that in such episodes the autonomous activity of the percipients' own associations and mental processes are creating the images he reports so clearly and so intensely. Almost always these percipients report that they felt calm and at ease, that the entity seems kind and benevolent; and a feeling of benevolence is another indicator of trance development.

Time distortion is still another indicator, and also another feature of many of the abduction cases where the suggestion that an abduction might be involved only came after someone realized that a large block of time could not be accounted for. In the clinical setting, the doctor sets up the proper conditions for the induction of trance; one of these sometimes is to create a boring state of mind. And many of the abductions and voyeur cases appear to be preceded by a similar routine state of mind. If in fact we are dealing with hypnotic, trancelike states, it would seem reasonable to expect that such percipients are right hemisphere dominant, and this might in fact be at least one potential way to test this theory.

In conclusion, it appears that even though UFO occupant and critter cases may not shed light on the question of extraterrestrial civilizations, they may prove to be useful towards understanding clinical and non-clinical mental states, particularly the "spontaneous" creation of trance states. It is also possible that some of these states are correlated with real, and in principle, measurable, physical changes in the environment.

Notes to Part 6

1. John Brent Musgrave, "The UFO Investigator As Counsellor and Healer," Flying Saucer Review, Vol. 22, No. 5, 1976, pp. 26-27.

2. R. Leo Sprinkle, "Hypnotic Time Regression Procedures in the Investigation of UFO Experiences," in Coral and Jim Lorenzen, Abducted! Confrontations with Beings from Outer Space, 1977, pp. 191-210.

3. Alvin H. Lawson, "What Can We Learn from Hypnosis of Imaginary Abductees?" in 1977 MUFON UFO Symposium Proceedings, pp. 107-135.

A. Milton H. Erickson, Ernest L. Rossi and Sheila I. Rossi, Hypnotic Realities: The Induction of Clinical Hypnosis and Forms of Indirect Suggestion, 1976

CATALOGUE OF OCCUPANTS AND CRITTERS

The following list contains all the occupant and critter cases within Canada that have come to my attention as of this writing. It should be emphasized that this list contains reports whose reliability and usefulness varies. Some, or many, are spurious.

In addition to assigning their arbitrary type, the list includes some of the key words used when filing UFO reports. At present I use just over 75 words, ranging from "abduction" to "water" as keys to identifying the patterns which may exist in the UFO phenomenon.

Type 0-insufficient information

Type 1-fly-by

Type 2-stopping for the view

Type 3-stroller - no UFO

Type 4-stroller - UFO

Type 5-tourist

Type 6-pit-stop

Type 7-peeping tom

Type 8-molester/contact

AM-air motion

APL:S-sighting made from airplane

APT: S-sighting made at airport

AR-animal reaction

EE:P/D-electromagnetic effect: power/dimming

EE:R/TV-electromagnetic effect: radio/television

FOL-following

FF-force field

FOR-formation (more than one UFO)

IV-internal view

LR-light ray

PROJECT MAGNET

MIB-"men in black"

MP/H-mock plane/helicopter

O-odor/smell

PT-physical trace

PE-physiological effect (injury, headache, etc.)

PH-photograph

PS-psychic

RES-residue

ROT-rotation/spin

RCAF+I-military involvement/investigation

RCAF+S-military sighting

RCMP+I-police involvement/investigation

RCMP+S-police sighting

SCI-scientist/engineer made sighting

S/N-sound

SD-structural detail on UFO

T/H-temperature/heat associated with UFO (other than trace)

TIME-time lapse reported

V/C vapour or cloud

V-voices heard

W-water

01 autumn 1796, sunrise-New Mines, Nova Scotia. A young girl and two men observed 15 "sailing ships" flying through the air to the east above the Bay of Fundy. "Portholes" could be seen as well as a man forward with his hand stretched out. (Type I: FOR, SD, W)

02 1912 morning- Six year old boy living on farm in contact with "space men". Round craft, which looked something like a "helicopter". Short men with round feet, no knees or elbows, examined him and communicated "telepathically". (Type 8: MP/H, PS, SD)

03 Aug. 1914, early even.- Eight people observed a globular shaped object above the water at Georgia Bay, Ontario. The object was described as being 9 feet by 12 feet, with small men busy with a hose going into the water. After about 10 minutes the occupants noticed them, and took off in a hurry with one of the small men clinging to the rail. (Type 6: AR, IV, S/N, SD, V/C, W)

04 Winter 1924, 0600- While going out to do morning chores, woman observed a "little green man" walking around near a slew on her Saskatchewan farm. The entity went into the "ship" which took off. (Type A: W)

05 12 June 1929, 2300- Fermeneuve, Quebec. Man on horseback observed

a dark object with a yellow light and four or five dwarflike beings running about near it. Their "childlike piercing voices" scared both him and his horse.

06 Oct. 1932, 1800- Joliette, Quebec. Five people witnessed an 8 feet tall giant dressed in white walking like "astronauts on the moon" as they drove by in their car. (Type 3)

07 Summer 1935, early morning- Nipawin, Saskatchewan. A young woman and two men observed an oval shaped object supported by six legs sitting in muskeg and woods. About a dozen silver suited small men observed for 30 minutes going up and down ladder like structure. When site inspected a day later square imprints and burnt marking observed and photographed. Photographs subsequently lost. (Type 6: PT, PH, SD)

08 1948- Man observed a disc like object land on ground near Svastika, Ontario. An entity left the object and collected samples of vegetation. The object transmitted a "force field" which pushed the witness to the ground. (Type 5: FF)

09 1948- Same witness as case 8 observed an object on the ground. Three entities, who smiled at him, were observed outside the craft A police patrol saw a light in a nearby woods, but couldn't approach it because of an "invisible wall". (Type H: FF, RCMP+S)

10 2 July 1950, evening- Sawbill Bay, Ontario. Couple observed disc with portholes, hatch covers and hoop-shaped object on top which rotated slowly. Slight humming could be heard as tiny men moved like robots with a hose extending to the lake. Residue left on water after object flew off. (Type 6: AM, RES, S/N, SD, W)

11 late July 1950, evening-Same man as in case 10 plus male companion observed similar "saucer" above Sawbill Bay. Only observed for a few seconds as the hose was reeled in. The craft took off with a high pitched whine, with one entity hanging aboard. (Type 6: S/N, SD, W)

12 2 Sept. 1950, late evening-Man observed the silhouette of a person between beach and himself at the end of Harmon Air Force Base runway. When he investigated, he saw a flash and felt his hand burn. (Type 0: PE, RCAF+|, RCAF+S)

13 June 1954, mid-morning-A man was pumping water on his farm near Harptree, Saskatchewan, when he heard a droning sound like a Honda motorcycle. Then he saw a transparent disc-shaped object about 50 feet in diameter. He could see two men inside with helmets and goggles working a stick shift Flew between man and nearby shed. (Type I: AM, IV, S/N, SD)

14 2 July 1954, afternoon-A Garson, Ontario miner saw three entities 13 feet tall descend from a "space ship". They were described as "built in much the same manner as the ship" which was 25 feet in diameter. This craft had electronic ear-like spurs on its top, and 3 sets of arms with claws and six legs. He claimed the ship transmitted radio messages, and the occupants had a "hypnotic power" over him. Both the Ontario Provincial Police and military described this case as a hoax.

PROJECT MAGNET

(Type A: EE:R/TV, RCAF+|, RCMP+1, SD)

15 7 Aug. 19541, 1930-Two young boys observed a sudden flash of light, accompanied by a high whining sound (like the buzzing of bees) on a farm near Hemingford, Quebec. They could see a round, glowing object above ground which lowered a square shaft to the ground to hold it up. A circular door opened, and a huge 7 feet tall white colored entity emerged. The entity, dressed in a black "rubber suit" stood looking at the boys until they fled. Their mother investigated and observed a globular bubble. The object took off an hour or more later with a brilliant orange glow. (Type H: AR, PT, S/N, SD)

16 aut. 1954 or 1955, daytime-Man driving car near Calgary, Alberta observed a silvery disc. Inside he could see a man with long black hair and leather jacket. Only observed a few seconds. Man was later committed to mental hospital where he claimed entity was Jesus Christ. (Type I)

17 3 Oct. 1954, 1600-A miner was canoeing on Lac Ia Pause, Quebec, when he felt a prickling sensation on his back. He could see the water "boiling" near him, and looked up to see a bronze colored oval object. The object was 30 feet by 12 feet, and flew silently by. The object stopped, and two small men with transparent head gear, and white rubber suits emerged. They gathered vegetation and returned to the craft after about 10 minutes. Before leaving they "gargled" some words. They had steel-like claws. (Type S: AM, PE, SD, V, W)

18 winter 1955, 2330-A young woman and her fiance observed a "ghost" from the balcony of a home in Ste-Therese, Quebec. The human looking form was described as 8 feet tall, with white glowing skin. A beam of light illuminated the entity as well as the ground beside. (Type 3: LR)

19 mid-Aug. 1958, 2245-Woman noticed a patch of blue light outside window of farm home at Bells Corner, Ontario. She went outside to investigate with her grown son. When she walked up to patch of light she observed a small person about size of six year old child. The light seemed to come from its eyes. Her son, who stood close by, could only see the blue light. (Type 7)

20 1960s-Rumors from native people that occupants, size of young children, observed in northern Manitoba. These beings were poking in the mud, and carried a rod which could be used to shoot a beam of light. They wore close-fitting coverall type suits with some kind of hood. Observed to board vehicles which then took off. (Type 5)

21 1960s, afternoon-Near Lac St-Jean, Quebec, a Montreal engineer came upon a machine shaped like a top, with an inward sloping circular superstructure supported on legs. He climbed inside and inspected the interior. While inside, the occupants returned and communicated, discussing their method of propulsion. (Type 8: IV, S/N, SD, V)

22 8 Aug. 1961, 0330-Wetaskiwin, Alberta. Couple woke up to observe two small entities standing by their bed. Both witnesses felt paralyzed, but could hear the two entities talking. Both wore "helmets" and 2-piece suits, and were "beautifully proportioned". When the entities disappeared, both witnesses could again move. At the same time a neighbor next door observed a 25 feet bluish globe hovering by their home, which slowly lifted off the ground and accelerated to the north. (Type 7: S/N, V)

23 31 May 1962, 2100-While hanging cloths out to dry, a Montreal, Quebec woman observed a barrel shaped object, "ketchup red" colored, flying no more than 450 feet away. The object was 8 or 9 feet high, and 6 feet wide. Two entities could be seen inside through two round portholes. Observed perhaps two minutes. (Type I: IV)

24 19 Sept. 1963, 2000-Many children in a Saskatoon, Saskatchewan schoolyard observed a bright light hover over a nearby field. A "box" was dropped. When they went to investigate, a 10 feet tall man appeared, held out his hands and came towards them. He was dressed like a "monk" and appeared transparent at times. (Type H: RCMP+|)

25 20 Sept. 1963, evening-The same children as in case 24 returned to the playground and saw the same object hover over the field. They thought they saw a man lying on the ground because they saw "arms and legs move". (Type 0)

26 late 1960s, morning-Man on farm near Didsbury, Alberta, looked up from work to see small silver suited entity floating in air immediately in front of him. Entity floated to craft, which then took off. (Type 4)

27 July 1965, 2200-Two young women in Rosemont, Quebec were out walking when they heard a strange noise like "roller skates". When they looked in the direction of the noise, they saw the torso (bottom part of figure not visible) of a beautiful smiling man with deep penetrating eyes. Both women felt in a trance for perhaps 5 minutes. (Type 7: S/N)

28 end July 1965, 1630-Three young boys observed a strange binocular-shaped craft zig-zag down from sky near Trois-Rivieres, Quebec. After the craft disappeared behind a cliff, they went to investigate. A 5 feet tall red-colored entity, with a flat elongated head was observed. The craft was made of two cylinders about 5 feet tall, connected by supporting rods. (Type A)

29 Aug. 1965, 2130-A couple parked in a car near an Ottawa, Ontario reservoir saw a bright light which lit up the whole area. The glowing object approached the reservoir, with A "searchlights" shining to the ground. The craft stopped close to the surface of the water, and a sliding door opened, through which three figures could be seen. At that point the couple drove away in fright. (Type 6?: LR, SD, W)

30 spring 1966, 0200-Family was asleep at home in Wetaskiwin, Alberta when

4 year old son yelled out "Who's that standing in the hall?" Father in bedroom opposite that of son also observed the torso (bottom part invisible) of human looking entity which wore grey colored suit like skin diver. Image disappeared after about 5 seconds. While visible, the man said he felt "relaxed." (Type 7)

31 Early April 1966, 0545-Six year old boy in Calgary, Alberta heard truck noises outside. Looked outside and saw three discs land in nearby field. Small entities emerged who appeared to be looking around and discussing something. They scrambled aboard the "saucer" which took off to the north. (Type 4?: FOR)

32 4 April 1966-UFO, 20 feet in diameter reported to have landed near airfield at Trenton, Ontario. Two small entities emerged, and reentered when service police attempted to get near. (Type H: APT:S)

33 Early summer 1966, night-Woman awakened from sleep at Qualicum Beach, British Columbia. Heard a humming, like a motor, and observed a large, luminous sphere in the garden outside. Then saw a tall human figure in silvery metallic clothes. The figure raised his hand, and a ray of light came from the hand and hit her upper body. Then the light, sound and figure disappeared instantly. Her husband and young son were asleep nearby. (Type 7: LR, S/N)

34 autumn 1966, daytime-Near Island Lake, Manitoba. Stories that at same time dogs in community barking, young children claimed that little men about 3-1/2 feet tall, dressed in silver suits, gave them candy which lasted for days. (Type 8: AR)

35 13 June 1967, 0230-Miner at Caledonia, Ontario saw two craft hovering about 12 feet above the ground near the mine. One was cigar shaped, perhaps 30 feet long, with windows on the side. The other was disc shaped, about 15 feet in diameter. Three small men about 4 feet tall could be seen under the larger craft. They seemed to be picking up things from the ground. When the man returned with a friend the entities were gone, but the two craft could still be seen. Later an oily residue and marks were discovered. (Type 5: FOR, MIB, PT, RES, SD)

36 July 1967, afternoon-Eleven year old boy followed by UFO as he rode his bicycle at St-Stanislas-de-Kotska, Quebec. The bottom was made of "glass" and three small, black colored, entities could be seen inside. (Type 1: FOL, IV)

37 mid Aug. 1967, evening-Family in Welland, Ontario, observed two lights travelling across sky in about three minutes time. Through binoculars, "figures" could be seen in one of the lights. The lights were estimated to be 1/2 mile away. (Type 1: FOR)

38 12 Aug. 1967, late evening-Dozen teenagers claim they saw a "huge black monster" descend from a lighted craft near Richibucto, New Brunswick. The figure was dressed in black, with black face and goggles. (Type H: RCMP+|)

39 14 Aug. 1967-Woman from St. Charles, New Brunswick, reported sighting a similar type critter as case 38. (Type O: RCMP+|)

PROJECT MAGNET

40 15 Aug. 1967, 0730-Young boy was outside with his dog on farm near Port Perry, Ontario when he heard a strange oscillating sound. He went over nearby hill and saw a disc shaped craft about 12 feet in diameter with 4 legs about 5 or 6 feet long. The object was hovering over the ground. On a platform around the perimeter were seated 8 to 10 little men, perhaps 3 feet tall. They were brown with tight fitting cloths. Later a slightly depressed circular ring about 12 feet in diameter was discovered where the craft was observed. (Type 6?: AR, PT, S/N, SD)

41 23 Aug. 1967, early morning-Man driving near Joyceville, Ontario when he saw a green light in nearby field. He stopped and observed huge saucer shaped craft, and two 4 feet tall little men nearby. They appeared to be working on the machine. When they noticed him, the two jumped into the saucer which took off quickly. (Type 6: RCMP+|)

42 17 Sept. 1967, 0200-Eight feet tall "space man" observed near Langley, British Columbia. Pink colored with scaly skin. (Type 0)

43 30 Oct. 1967, 2100-While walking home near Melfort, Saskatchewan, man observed an object, perhaps 50 feet long, through which he could see a square light about 4 feet high and 16 feet long. Suddenly a bright spotlight came on, and he saw 3 small entities emerge. The 3 had headgear, and were dressed in green uniforms. The craft took off with the passengers still on ground. Some broken trees discovered next morning. (Type A: LR, PT)

44 17 Nov. 1967, 1800-Young boy arrived home in Calgary, Alberta in state of shock. Remembered being "chased" by a flying saucer. Subsequently, in a dream he recalled being taken aboard the craft by crocodile-skinned entities who examined him on an operating table. (Type 8: S/N)

45 late July 1968, 1845-Many children on farm near St Bruno, Quebec saw a cloud come down from the sky. The "Virgin Mary" emerged and spoke to them about peace and brotherhood. (Type 8: V/C, V)

46 26 July 1968, 1500-Two young boys were riding their bicycles near the airport at Riviere-du-Loup, Quebec. They stopped near a hanger and noticed a grey skinned robot-like entity about 100 feet away, and about 3 feet tall. When spotted, it ran away, joined by a companion. (Type 3: APT:S)

47 28 July 1968, 2100-Five children watched two UFOs near St-Stanislas-de-Kotska, Quebec. One landed 1,000 feet away, while the other remained in the sky. When they went outside to investigate, the light from their flashlight lit up the head of a 4 feet tall entity. It opened and closed its mouth, but made no noise. The children fled to the house. The critter grunted as it knocked at the window pane. The UFO left with a red glow. (Type 4: FOR, PT, S/N, V)

48 28 July 1968, near midnight-Man, his wife and two children were awakened by the barking of their dog at Upton, Quebec. When he arose to investigate,

he saw a sparkling, rotating "cloud" in the yard. It flew just over him and went to nearby field. About 12 feet in diameter, it was dark on the bottom, but luminous on top. The cows in the field were being chased by 4 or 5 small entities, perhaps 3 feet tall with heads shaped like bottles. As the UFO flew above them, they disappeared. The cattle seemed ill for weeks afterwards. (Type SY: AR, ROT, V/C)

49 4 Aug. 1968, 0500-Three young men walking in Montreal, Quebec noticed a 3 feet tall "monkey man" in the shadows. The "monkey" had long curving arms and hunched over as if carrying a heavy weight. It made a tremendous leap, and then disappeared. (Type 3)

50 6 Aug. 1968, 2130-Four adolescent boys were outside, when they heard the dog barking furiously and saw it tugging on the rope, near Ste-Gertrude, Quebec. They heard a creaking sound, and saw a 4 feet tall luminous entity leave the hedge where the dog was barking. It had large shoulders and long arms which hung down. It instantly disappeared in front of them. (Type 3: AR, S/N)

51 29 Aug 01 Sept. 1968, afternoon-Four days in a row, group of children saw a 4 feet tall red colored dwarf with black beard near a bolder at the Coleraine, Quebec, cemetery. A roaring sound was heard nearby, and a 30 feet wide, blue, white and red UFO observed in an excavation near the bolder. The UFO left a trail of smoke. (Type Q?: S/N, V/C)

52 14 Sept. 1968, 2200-Two young women in Drummondville, Quebec saw a "strange" man walking on the street in front of them. When it spotted them, it stopped. They looked away for an instant, and it had disappeared, even though the street light illuminated a wide area. A nearby dog, normally quiet, was barking furiously. (Type 3: AR)

53 15 Sept. 1968, 2015-Same two women as case 52, plus two more, noticed a 4 feet tall entity, surrounded by light on a gravel road behind house of one of them in Drummondville, Quebec. It stopped when it noticed them, and "disappeared". (Type 3)

54 21 Sept. 1968, 2000-Two young girls in Coaticook, Quebec saw an entity. Several people claim to have observed an object which emitted flashes of orange, red, and green. Some tracks were found, and a burnt circle. (Type O: PT)

55 28 Sept. 1968, 2145-Green rectangular shaped "cloud" observed in sky above Asbestos, Quebec by 4 adults. The cloud became brighter, and after a couple of minutes a luminous "saucer" emerged. Two human figures were observed to "walk in space". (Type 0: RCMP+I, V/C)

56 Nov. 1968, 0230-Pilot, co-pilot, and navigator saw a disc shaped object as they flew about 150 miles north of Yellowknife, N.W.T. When the pale blue object was closest, they could make out a figure inside. (Type I: APL:S)

57 1969-Two men observed disc shaped object while driving in Calgary, Alberta. As it flew by, they saw an occupant inside. (Type I)

58 26 April 1969, evening-Young man was walking the dog in Calgary, Alberta, when the dog suddenly stopped. The man observed a circular object about 30 feet in diameter with 3 pulsating red lights on the top. A sweet-bitter smell made him a bit nauseous. Two taller than normal entities were outside the craft. (Type Q?: AR, O)

59 June 1969, 2130-Near Overton, Nova Scotia, a woman noticed a light above a swampy area behind her home. She saw a machinelike object with a rim around, and "someone walking around the rim." A constant drumming sound could be heard, and from time to time a puff of smoke came from the object. The light was observed to go off into the sky. (Type 6?: S/N, SD, V/C)

60 1 July 1969, 0615-Man walking through building at Olds, Alberta, when he heard clattering outside. He looked out window and saw a large green cylindrical object descend from a dense cloud. Only 50 feet away, he could see two figures inside. An impression was noticed in the ground where it had been. (Type 2: IV, PT, V/C)

61 summer 1969, 2100-Group of adolescents were by reservoir near Trois-Rivieres, Quebec late July or early August. One of the two cars would not start, even though the battery and gas had been checked. While one group left to get help, three remained behind. They saw a light about 20 feet above the reservoir; and then 7 or 8 entities looking like "Snowmen" floating in the air towards them. The 3 could feel the car heat up, and shudder, panicked and hid in the car under the blankets. They then heard footsteps on the roof of the car. Later, marks were found on the roof. Their ordeal lasted an hour. (Type 8?: EE:P/D, PT, S/N, T/H)

62 14 Sept. 1969, 1700-Seven year old boy saw two small entities near Beauharnois, Quebec. They emerged from a small silver ship through a hatch. They were green colored, and moved like robots as they gathered rocks and plants before returning to the machine. (Type 5: S/N)

63 13 Oct. 1969, 2200-Round object, which made a kind of whistling sound, flew over Vancouver, British Columbia. "Numerous men" thought to be observed within by man who reported sighting. (Type 1: S/N)

64 1 Jan. 1970, 0500-Nurse on duty observed a glowing disc-shaped object approximately 40 feet from hospital in Cowichan, British Columbia. Inside the transparent dome she could see two beautifully pro portioned figures in front of an "instrument panel." After taking off from side of building, other people saw the craft, but not the entities. (Type 2: IV, SD)

65 early 1970, 2230-Man in Brandon, Manitoba woke up to see two identical white colored beings looking at him through living room window. He tried to get up but felt paralyzed from a devise held in arm of one of the entities. His wife was in kitchen at time and unaware of what was going on. (Type 7: PE)

66 end Feb. 1970, noon-Young boy in grade 2 was returning to school from

lunch in Terrace, British Columbia, when he met a "little green man." The green-ish colored entity had a small head, but large feet. The boy could see "a round thing" from which he thought the entity had come. The critter jabbered at him, and gave him a patty of strange material. (Type 8: V)

67 11 July 1970, 2100-Three young women driving near airport at Trois-Rivieres, Quebec, saw a white smoke cloud above the road. Inside they saw a thin figure of a humanlike entity. They then drove through the cloud and saw nothing. (Type Q?: V/C)

68 9 June 1971, 2050-Woman near Rosedale, Alberta, noticed a bright light through the window. Outside she saw a transparent rectangular object about 200 feet away, and 3 entities in tightly fitting green suits. The entity outside the craft appeared to be picking up rocks. Her dog refused to go nearer, and dragged her back to the house. Burnt vegetation discovered. (Type 5: AR, IV, PT)

69 12 July 1971, 2300-Young man was returning home near Notre-Dame-du-Nord, Quebec, when he saw something white speed across the road. Soon he noticed a human shaped "transparent" being who seemed unaware of the wit-ness. The entity was white, and had a pointed nose. (Type 3)

70 4 Nov. 1972, 1645-Woman washing dishes in remote cottage near Clyde, Alberta, began to see silvery shiny discs all around her house. She looked through window and saw the torso (bottom part not visible) of a beautifully proportioned, golden haired being. The being's eyes were brilliant gold, with beams of light that were blinding. Later that night she had a "dream" where she was taken to the moon by the being. (Type 7)

71 28 Nov. 1972, 1030-A group of children near Sarre, Quebec, noticed a cloud-like object descend to earth. Three small, square shaped black colored "divers" emerged. One entity came towards the house. The principal witness, a boy of 9 years, went into the house to get a hockey stick to beat it off. When he returned outside, the entities were going back into the "cloud". (Type H: V/C)

72 29 July 1973, 2100-As university professor and his wife were driving near Ottawa, Ontario, they noticed a bright globe of light. As it passed near them, they could see three humanoid silhouettes through three oblong portholes. The object flew over the car. (Type I: IV, LR, SD)

73 6 Oct. 1973, early and late morning-Couple near St-Mathias, Quebec, noticed a bright "spotlight" on their farm just after midnight. Later in morning they saw a domed object on the ground, from which emerged a smaller object. Five small figures were observed. Later the grass was found to be flattened and discolored, as well as strange imprints. (Type 6?: LR, PT, V/C)

74 29 Oct. 1973, 2200-Man walking his dog in Toronto, Ontario park when he saw a bluish-green fluorescent light forming a circle of light on a brick wall. Inside the circle of light he saw a "TV screen" with images, including that of enti-

ties. Communications ensued between the man and the entities on the screen. Dog frightened, and man became physically ill. (Type 8: AR, PE)

75 18 Nov. 1973, evening-Four young women driving in car near Tracy, Quebec noticed a ball of light which changed brightness and distance from them. Later they passed through a cloud or mist on the road; and further down the road they noticed a strange "man" no more than 5 feet tall brushing along the road, apparently unaware of the traffic. (Type O?: V/C)

76 22 Nov. 1973, 0200-Woman, unable to sleep, was in her kitchen in Joliette, Quebec, when she saw a "beautiful creature" staring through the window. It had a round head and bright glowing eyes. It was surrounded by a halo of bright light. Her husband was asleep in the next room. When he examined the ground outside by the window, he discovered a dog "scared to death" nearby. (Type 7= AR)

77 31 Dec. 1973, 2230-Man driving east of Medicine Hat, Alberta saw a bright light in rearview mirror. The light was like a revolving light on train, except no trains on that section of road. Then he noticed an 8 feet tall man running in a ditch alongside, even though he was driving at least 60 mph. The entity came up to the truck and placed his hands on the roof and hood, and then disappeared. (Type 3)

78 April 1974, 0515-Woman looked out of kitchen window in Timmins, Ontario, and saw a red light in the sky. The object moved closer, and then stopped. An entity emerged from a hatch, and moved toward the top of the craft After about two minutes, the UFO moved to the south and out of view. (Type 6?)

79 25 June 1974, early morning-While watching TV near Drummondvllle, Quebec, a man heard a throbbing noise. He looked out the window and saw a reddish disc with a dome. He woke up his wife, and the two of them, watched through the morning as many entities were walking all around the trailer court which had just opened, and had no other residents. Six feet tall entities, with red horizontal "neon lights" across their chests floated around, looking at tool sheds, and other structures around their home. Three rings were found the next day in the nearby field. As well, several pieces of a strange white substance were discovered where some of the entities had been wandering. (Type H: PT, RES, S/N)

80 July 1975, late evening-Man was driving near Radium Hot Springs, British Columbia, when he saw a no feet diameter disc shaped object. The object had rectangular windows on the side, and lights shining down. He could also hear a swishing kind of sound. A shadow could be seen inside, through one of the windows, as if there was someone inside. By his watch, he was there more than an hour, but only seemed like minutes. (Type 2: LR, S/N, SD, TIME)

81 7 Oct. 1975, 2100-Man on farm near Bracebridge, Ontario, drove out to investigate orange glow in the sky. His headlights illuminated a 12 to 14 feet diameter oval object on the ground. He turned the car around, and further up the road he saw a 4 or 5 feet tall entity jump over a fence. While the UFO was around, the

TV lost its sound and picture. (Type H: EE:R/TV)

82 9 Oct. 1975, 0600-While letting out the cat, a North Bay, Ontario woman saw a 3-1/2 feet tall creature. It appeared to be running down the street in "slow motion" trailing an aura of sparkling white behind. (Type 3)

83 14 Oct. 1975, 0530-Woman driving home from work near Peers, Alberta, noticed a "cattle truck" on road ahead of her. When she passed it, she could see a large oval object, with a superstructure, and two stationary silver suited entities holding rods stiffly in their hands. (Type 6?: SD)

84 Nov. 1975, 1800-Woman walking in Montreal, Quebec, noticed a brilliant disc shaped object in the sky. Through large rectangular windows, she saw moving shadows which could have been entities. The object then took off. (Type 2: SD)

85 29 July 1976, 0110-Woman in Sabrevois, Quebec, arose to attend to one of her children. Outside she could see a ball of light. She went to the next room to wake her husband, and saw two entities in the entranceway. The entities were bright globes of light atop "legs." While she searched for binoculars, her husband arose to see two bright globes of light merge into one like an electrical sputtering. (Type 7)

86 6 Aug. 1976, 1000-A family driving in Gaspesie, Quebec, on a foggy day found their car being paced by a red spotlight. Later their car engine stopped, and headlights went off, and car inside began to heat up. When outside, they later saw a huge oval object with windows, and entities with large eyes which frightened all of them. (Type H: EE:P/D, LR, PE, S/N, T/H)

87 6 Jan. 1977, 0115-Woman looked out of apartment in Montreal, Quebec, and saw a disc shaped object land on the roof of a nearby building. Two tall helmeted entities walked on the roof. They got back into the disc, and it took off. A circle, and footprints reported in the ice. (Type H?: PTI

88 6 April 1977, 1900-A disc shaped object, perhaps 40 feet long, with a row of windows observed in Ste-Dorothee, Quebec. The object made a buzzing sound, as it was seen to go to nearby field. Two boys went to investigate, and saw it graze the surface of a pond. As it passed over the pond, the water evaporated with a sound like water on a hot surface. As the object remained by the pond, they could see an entity in front of the disc. Later "footprints" were discovered. (Type A: PT, S/N, W)

89 4 Feb. 1978, 2200-Grade 6 student out walking in Scarborough, Ontario, when he heard a wavering sharp siren-type sound, and looked up to see a saucer-shaped object hovering above the ground. He observed movement that looked like creatures through the dome portion. (Type I: S/N, SD)

90 17 Feb. 1978-Humanoid reported near Dollard-des-Ormeaux, Quebec. (Type 0)

PROJECT MAGNET

INDEX TO CATALOGUE

PROJECT MAGNET

FF: 8, 9.

FOR: 1, 31, 35, 37, 47.

IV: 3, 13, 21, 23, 36, 60, 64, 68, 72.

LR: 18, 29, 33, 43, 72, 73, 80, 86.MIB: 35.

MP/H: 2.O: 58.

PT: 7, 15, 35, 40, 43, 47, 54, 60, 61, 68, 73, 79, 87, 88.

PE: 12, 17, 65, 74, 86.

PH: 7.

PS: 2.

RES: 10, 35, 79.

ROT: 48.

RCAF+1: 12, 14.

RCAF+S: 12.

RCMP+1: 14, 24, 38, 39, 41, 55.

RCMP+S: 9.

SCI: 21, 72.

S/N: 3, 10, 11, 13, 15, 21, 22, 27, 33, 40, 44, 50, 51, 59, 61, 62, 63, 79, 80, 86, 88, 89.

SD: 1, 2, 3, 7, 10, 11, 13, 14, 15, 17, 21, 29, 35, 40, 59, 64, 72, 80, 83, 84, 89.

T/H: 61, 86.

TIME: 80.V/C: 3, 45, 48, 51, 55, 59, 60, 67, 71, 73, 75.

V: 5, 17, 21, 22, 45, 47, 66.

W: 1, 3, 4, 10, 11, 17, 29, 88.

CATALOGUE FOOTNOTES

1. Various US and Canadian newspapers.

2. Personal phone conversation; letter at Center for UFO Studies, Evanston, Illinois, USA.

3. Letters to APRO and Timothy Green Beckley; Coral and Jim Lorenzen. Flying Saucer Occupants, pp. I9-23. See footnotes to cases 10 and 11.4. Phone-in show. Radio station CJCA, Edmonton, Alberta. 31 May |976.

5. Henri Bordeleau, j'ai chasse les pilotes de soucoupes volantes, pp. 11-16.

6. Claude MacDuff et Philippe Blaquieve, OURANOS, No. 9, |972, p. ZA.

7. Personal communication. APRO Bulletin, Vol. 25, No. 9, March I977, pp. 17; Canadian UFO Report, Vol. 4, No. A, Summer I977, pp. 6-7; Flying Saucer Review, Vol. 22, No. 6, 1976, pp. 16-17. The date 1933 in these articles is incorrect.

8. UFO INFO (Belgium), juin 1977» P. 16.9. lbid.

10. The original article which appeared in the Steep Rock Echo was reprinted in FATE Magazine, February-March I952, pp. 68-72. See also: Harold T. Wilkins, Flying Saucers on the Attack, pp. 252-256; Frank Edwards, Flying Saucers—Serious Business, pp. 91-93; and, Coral and Jim Lorenzen, Flying Saucer Occupants, pp. 23-25.

The Lorenzen's point out that work done recently by Robert Badgley demonstrates that the article was written by Gordon Edwards as a joke, and that the whole affair was a hoax from the beginning. If this is true, it must cast severe doubt on the William Kiehl case (3) as well. This case is in many ways a carbon copy, and even though perporting to be much earlier, was in fact only reported in 1966, many years after the Sawbill Bay story was published in FATE.

11. Article in Steep Rock Echo. It might be worth mentioning that although the incident in case 10 has no mention of a dangling entity, this case does. Kiehl's 1914 case also speaks of an entity left behind on the out- side of the craft.

12. Project Blue Book Case #795.

13. Investigated by Dean Clausen, of the Saskatchewan Unidentified Phenomena Research organization. See also Saucers, Space 8 Science, No. 62, 1971,

pp. 12.

14. Sudbury Daily Star, Tuesday July 6, 195h. Project Blue Book Case #308h. Donald E. Keyhoe, The Flying Saucer Conspiracy, pp. 145-146.

15. Henri Bordeleau, j'ai chasse les pilotes de soucou es volantes, pp. 18-41. A slightly different version of what happened including a different date - 28 August 1954) is given in a report submitted to NICAP.

16. CAPIC Reports (date unknown).17. Jean Ferguson, Tout sur les Soucoupes Volantes, pp. 167-172.

18. Henri Bordeleau, j'ai chasse les pilotes de soucoupes volantes, pp. 43-46.

19. W.B. Smith and J.R. Buchanan, "The Bells Corner Mystery," Topside, June 1960, pp. 3-4.

20. Letter to APRO from Norway House, Manitoba.21. R.B. Leeming, "Encounter with a UFO," Flying Saucers. Mysteries of the Space Age, No. 92, June 1976, pp. 20-29. Wido Hoville has spoken with the author who now claims the article was purely fiction.

22. Report by Bill Holt, Edmonton UFO Society. Also letters to APRO and NICAP

23. Wido Hoville, "Les UFO's en Baril," UFO Quebec, No. 6, 1976, p. I2.24. Investigated by Saskatoon Unidentified Flying Objects Club. Mary Lou Guenther, "A Canadian Saucer Encounter," Interplanetary News Service, No. 10, 1964, pp. 4-5.25. Ibid.26. Personal communication.

27. Henri Bordeleau, j'ai chassegles pilotes de soucoupes volantes, pp. 46-52.

28. Ibid, pp. 55-60.29. Coral and Jim Lorenzen, Encounters with UFO Occupants, pp. 201-202.

30. Investigated by Bill Holt, Edmonton UFO Society.31. APRO files.32. Letter to NICAP.

33. Letter by Witness in Saga UFO Report, October 1977, pp. 76-77.34. Letter to NICAP.

35. Saucers, Space 8 Science, No. 49. Fall 1967, p. 9. CAPRO, Vol. 1, No. 1, January 1968.

Some investigators believe the witness was subsequently visited by the ubiquitous "Men in Black." See, for instance, Lawrence J. Fenwick, "Mysteries Follow Landing," Canadian UFO Report, Spring 1977, pp. 8-12; and Lawrence J. Fenwick, "Crisis or Solution?" The UFO Pulse Analyzer, No. 2, May 1977. PP- 2-13.

36. Henri Bordeleau, j'ai chasse les pilotes de soucoupes volantes, pp. 77-79; I103-109. Saucers, Space $ Science, No. 53, Fall I968, pp. 7-8. Gordon Creighton, "An Unprepossesing Creature Seen in Canada," Flying Saucer Review, Vol. 15, No. 3, May/June 1969, pp. 20-21. See also case 47.

37. Letter to APRO by witness.38. Moncton Times (New Brunswick), August 17, 1967.39. Ibid,40. Letter to APRO.41. Kingston Whig Standard (Ontario), August 24, 1967. Saucers, Space & Science, No. 49, Fall 1967, p. 9. A recent update is in The Toronto Sun (Ontario), January 8, 1978.42. Letter to APRO.43. Saskatoon UFO Bulletin. No. 2, January 1968.

44. W.K. Allan, "Crocodile-Skinned Entities at Calgary," Flying Saucer Review, Vol. 20, No. 6, 1974, pp. 25-26. B. Ann Slate, "Contactee Supplies New Clues to UFO Mystery," Saga UFO Report, Vol. 3, No. 1, April 1976, pp. 26-30; 44.45. Saucer News, No. 7H, Spring-Summer 1969, p. 34.

46. Henri Bordeleau, j'ai chasse les pilotes de soucoupes volantes, pp. 100-103.

47. Ibid, pp. 77-79; 103-109. Saucers, Space & Science, No. 53, Fall 1968, pp. 7-8. Gordon Creighton, "An Unprepossessing Creature Seen in Canada," Flying Saucer Review, Vol. 15, No. 3, May/June 1969, pp. 20-21. The witness in case 36 is one of the 5 children to witness this case.

48. Henri Bordeleau, j'ai chasse les pilotes de soucoupes volantes, pp. 114-123.

49. Ibid, pp. 125-128.

50. Ibid, pp. 128-136.

51. Saucers, Space & Science, No. 53, Fall 1968, p. 11.

52. Henri Bordeleau, j'ai chasse les pilotes de soucoupes volantes, pp. 145-146.

53. Ibid, pp. 146-148.54. Ted Phillips, Physical Traces Associated With UFO Sightings, p. 59. This is likely a fictitious case, mixing occupant case 52 in Drummondville, Quebec, with a different sighting in Coaticook, Quebec, which occurred on a different date. The original newspaper articles (for example in La Tribune, 9 Octobre 1968) appear next to each other.

55. Henri Bordeleau, j'ai chasse les pilotes de soucoupes volantes, pp. 159-163.

56. Jeff Holt, "Rencontre Avec un UFO dans le Grand Nord," UFO-Quebec, No. 4, 1975, P. |7.

57. Phone-in show, radio station CFCN, Calgary, Alberta, January 1977.

58. W.K. Allan, "Report from Alberta," Saucers, Space 7 Science, No. 62, 1971, p. 8.

59. Letter to APRO.60. CAPRO, Vol. 4, No. 1, pp. 5-6.

61. Philippe Blaquiere, "Les Humanoides de Trois-Rivieres," UFO-Quebec, No. 2, 1976, pp. 4-5.

62. Henri Bordeleau, j'ai chasse les pilotes de soucoupes volantes, pp. 172-181.

63. Letter to APRO by witness.

64. Letter to APRO. Coral and Jim Lorenzen, Encounters with UFO Occupants, pp.- 200; 391-392.

65. Letter to APRO by witness.66. John Magor, Our UFO Visitors, pp. 193-197.

67. Henri Bordeleau, j'ai chasse les pilotes de soucoupes volantes, pp. 185-190.

68. W.K. Allan, "Humanoids and Craft Seen at Rosedale," Flying Saucer Review. Case Histories, No. 10, June 1972, pp. 4-5.

69. Jean Ferguson, "Un Etre Transparent au Nez Pointu," UFO-Quebec, No. 13, 1977, p. 11.

70. Personaliinterview.

71. Jean Ferguson, "Les Humanoides carres de la Sarre," UFO-Quebec, No. 5, 1976, pp. 9-11.

72. Wido Hoville et Don Donderi, "CE Ill sur la Route 17," UFO-Quebec, No. 14, June 1978, pp. 19-20.73. Wido Hoville, "Un Atterrissage a Saint-Mathias de Chambly," UFO-Quebec, No. 1, 1975, pp. 6-9. APRO Bulletin, Vol. 23, No. 2, September/October 1974, pp. 1; 3-4.74. Investigated by Henry McKay.

75. Marc Leduc, "Les Observations du 18.11.73," UFO-Quebec, No. 3, 1975, pp. 4-7. Claude MacDuff, Le Proces des Soucoupes Volantes,pp. 173-178.

76. Wido Hoville, "Joliette. 1973," UFO-Quebec, No. 2, 1975, p. 7.77. Investigated by Bill Holt, Edmonton UFO Society.

78. Mitch Leblanc, "Occupant Sighting in Timmins," UFO Informer, Summer 1977, p. 7.

79. Marc Leduc, 'Un Atterrissage et des Humanoides a Drummondville, UFO-Quebec, No. 1, 1975, pp. 10-12. Claude MacDuff, Le Proces des Soucoupes Volantes, pp. 197-204.

80. John Magor, "Time Lost in 'Playground of Gods'," Canadian UFO Report, No. 26, Winter 1976-77, pp. 1-3.

81. John Cosway, "UFO Sighting Sours Sole Spectator," The Sunday Sun (Toronto, Ontario), October 23, 1975. Report by Henry McKay.

82. Don Gauthier, "Little People?" North Bay Nugget (Ontario), October 11, 1975.

83. Personal interview.

84. Philippe Blaquiere, "Observation dans le quartier Rosemont," UFO-Quebec, No. 12, 1977, p. 7.

85. Marc Leduc, "Sainte-Anne-de-Sabrevois," UFO-Quebec, No. 7, 1976, p. 10.

86. Jean Ferguson, "Enquetes en Abitibi et en Gaspesie," UFO-Quebec, No. 8, 1976, pp.- 5-6; 11.

87. Marc Leduc et Wido Hoville, "Un UFO sur une Maison," UFO-Quebec, No. 9, 1977, pp. 6-10. Howard Gontavnick, "UFO Lands on Montreal Roof Top," The UFO Researchers Newsletter, Vol. 1, No. 3, Winter 1976, pp. 6-7; 18.

88. Marc Leduc, "Les Observations de Ste.Dorothee," UFO-Quebec, No. 10, 1977, pp.- 7-9~

89. Investigated by Joe Muskat, and reported in CUFORN Summary for May—December 1978, CUFORN, Inc.

90. Canadian UFO Report Network. Report No. 2 (UFO Canada), March 1978. No follow-up has been reported.

PROJECT MAGNET

BIBLIOGRAPHY
Books

Poul Anderson, Is There Life on Other Worlds?, Crowell-Collier Press, New York, 1963.

Bill Barry, Ultimate Encounter, Pocket Books, New York, 1978.

Henri Bordeleau, J'ai perce le mystere des soucoupes volantes, Societe Nefer Enregistree, Montreal, 1969.

, J'ai chassegles pilotes de soucoupes volantes, Societe Nefer Enregistree, Montreal, 1971.

Charles Bowen, editor, The Humanoids. A Survey of World-Wide Reports of Landings of Unconventional Aerial Objects & Their Alleged Occupants, Neville Spearman, London, 1969.

——Encounter Cases from Flying Saucer Review, Signet Books, New York, 1977.

Ronald N. Bracewell, The Galactic Club: Intelligent Life in Outer Space, Stanford Alumni Association, Stanford, California, 1974.

Arthur Bray, Science, the Public and the UFO, Bray Book Service, Ottawa, Ontario, 1967.

C. Maxwell Cade and Delphine Davis, The Taming of the Thunder Bolts: The Science and Superstition of Ball Lightning, Abelard-Schuman, London, 1969.

James L. Christian, editor, Extra-Terrestrial Intelligence: The First Encounter, Prometheus Books, Buffalo, New York, 1975.

Jerome Clark and Loren Coleman, The Unidentified: Notes Toward Solving the UFO Mystery, Warner Paperbacks, New York, 1975.

Edward U. Condon, Scientific Director, Final Report of the Scientific Study of Unidentified Flying Objects, E.P. Dutton S Co., New York, 1969.

Steven J. Dick, Plurality of Worlds and Natural Philosophy: An Historical Study of the Origins of Belief in Other Worlds and Extraterrestrial Life, Ph.D thesis, Department of History and Philosophy of Science, Indiana University, Bloomington, 1977.

Frank Edwards, Flying Saucers—Serious Business, Bantam Books, New York, 1966.

Milton H. Erickson, Ernest L. Rossi, and Shelia I. Rossi, Hypnotic Realities: The Induction of Clinical Hypnosis and Forms of Indirect Suggestion, Irvington Publishers, New York, 1976.

Jean Ferguson, Tout sur les soucoupes volantes, Lemeac, Ottawa, Ontario, 1972.

John G. Fuller, The Interrupted Journey: Two Lost Hours "Aboard a Flying Saucer, Dial Press, New York, 1966.

Gavin Gibbons, They Rode in Space Ships, The Citadel Press, New York, 1957.

Jesse E. Gordon, editor, Handbook of Clinical and Experimental Hypnosis, Macmillan Company, New York, 1967.

David Haisell, The Missing Seven Hours, PaperJacks, Markham, Ontario, 1978.

Hans Holzer, The UFOnauts: New Facts on Extraterrestrial Landings, Fawcett Pub-lications, Greenwich, Connecticut, 1976.

J. Allen Hynek, The UFO,Experience. A Scientific Inquiry, Henry Regnery, Chicago, 1972.

David Michael Jacobs, The UFO Controversy in America, Indiana University Press, Bloomington, 1975.

Stephen Jenkins, The Undiscovered Country: Adventures into Other Dimensions, Neville Spearman, Suffolk, 1977.

C. G. Jung, Flying Saucers: A Modern Myth of Things Seen in the Skies (1958), inVolume 10 of The Collected Works of C.G. Jung, Princeton University Press, Princeton, New Jersey, 1975.

John A. Keel, UFOs: Operation Trojan Horse, G.P. Putnam's Sons, New York, 1970.

Philip J. Klass, UFOs Explained, Random House, New York, 1974.Coral and Jim Lorenzen, Flying Saucer Occupants, Signet Books, New_York, 1967.

——Encounters with UFO Occupants, Berkley Medallion Books, New York, 1976.

——Abducted! Confrontations with Beings from Outer Space, Berkley Medallion Books, New York, 1977.

Claude MacDuff, Le proces des soucoupes volantes, Editions Quebec-Amerique, Montreal,'1975.

John Magor, Our UFO Visitors, Hancock House, Saanichton, British Columbia, 1977.

Magoroh Maruyama and Arthur Harkins, editors, Cultures Beyond the Earth,

Vintage Books, New York, 1975.

M. Minnaert, The Nature of Light & Colour in the Open Air, translated by H.M. Kremer-Priest, Dover Publications, New York, 1954.

Michael A. Persinger and Gyslaine F. Lafreniere, §pace-Time Transients and Un-usual Events, Nelson-Hall, Chicago, 1977.

Ted Phillips, compiler, Physical Traces Associated with UFO Sightings, Center for UFO Studies, Evanston, Illinois, 1975.

D.H. Rawcliffe, Illusions and Delusions of the Supernatural and the Occult, Dover Publications, New York, 1959.

Ian Ridpath, Messages from the Stars: Communication and Contact with Extrater-restrial Life, Harper & Row, New York, 1978.

Helen Ross, Behaviour and Perception in Strange Environments, George Allen & Unwin, London, 197h.

Alfred Roulet, The Search for Intelligent Life in Outer Space, translated and edited by William A. Packer, Berkley Medallion Books, New York, 1977.

N.A. Rynin, Interplanetary Flight and Communication. Vol. 1, No. 1. Dreams, Legends, and Early Fantasies, Leningrad, 1928. translated from the Russian. NASA, U.S. Department of Commerce, Washington, D.C., 1970.

Carl Sagan, editor, Communication with Extraterrestrial Intelligence (CETI), MIT Press, Cambridge, Massachusetts, 1973.

Michael Kelly Schutz, Organizational Goals and Support-Seeking Behavior: A Comparative Study of Social Movement Organizations in the UFO'(Flying Saucer? Field, Ph.D thesis, Department of Sociology, Northwestern University, Evanston, Illinois, 1973.

I. S. Shklovskii and Carl Sagan, Intelligent Life in the Universe, Holden-Day, San Francisco, 1966.

John Sladek, The New Apocrypha: A Guide to Strange Sciences and Occult Beliefs, Stein and Day, New York, 1973.

Marcia S. Smith, Life Beyond Earth, Coles Publishing, Toronto, 1978.

Susy Smith, Strangers from Space: An Introduction to the Enigma of Flying Saucers, Manor Books, New York, 1977.

Warren Smith, The Book of Encounters, Zebra Books, New York, 1978.

Herbert Spiegel and David Spiegel, Trance and Treatment. Clinical Uses of Hypnosis , Basic Books, New York, 1978.

Ray Stanford, Fatima Prophecy, Association for the Understanding of Man, Austin, Texas, 1974.

Brad Steiger, Revelations: The Divine Fire, Prentice Hall, Englewood Cliffs, New Jersey, 1973.

———Alien Meetings, Ace Books, New York, 1978.

Jack Stoneley and A.T. Lawton, Is Anyone Out There? Warner Paperbacks, New York, 1974.

Herbet Joseph Strentz, A Survey of Press Coverage of Unidentified Flying Objects, 1947-1966, Ph.D thesis, Department of Journalism, Northwestern University, Evanston, Illinois, 1970.

P. A. Sturrock, Evaluation of the Condon Report on the Colorado UFO Project, Stanford University Institute for Plasma Research Report No. 599, Stanford University, Stanford, California, October 1974.

Walter Sullivan, We Are Not Alone. The Search for Intelligent Life on Other Worlds, revised edition, McGraw-Hill, New York, 1963.

David Tansley, Omens of Awareness: Startling Parallels Between UFO Phenomenaand the Expanding Consciousness of Man, Neville Spearman, Suffolk, 1977.

G.M. Tovmasyan, editor, Extraterrestrial Civilizations , translated from the Russian, Israel Program for Scientific Translations, Jerusalem, 1967.

Montague Ullman, Stanley Krippner and Alan Vaughan, Dream Telepathy, Macmillan, New York, 1973.

Jacques Vallee, Passport to Magonia: From Folklore to Flying Saucers, Henry Regnery, Chicago, 1969.

———The Invisible College: What a Group of Scientists Has Discovered About UFO Influences on the Human Race, E.P. Dutton S Co., New York, 1975.

Everett Richard Walter, The Study of Unidentified Flying Objects and Its Adoption Within the Community College Curriculum, Ph.D thesis, Department of Education, Nova University, Fort Lauderdale, Florida, 1977.

Travis Walton, The Walton Experience, Berkley Medallion Books, New York, 1978.

David Webb, 1973 - Year of the Humanoids: An Analysis of the Fall, 1973 UFO/ Humanoid Wave, 2nd edition, Center for UFO Studies, Evanston, Illinois, 1976.

Harold T. Wilkins, Flying Saucers on the Attack, Citadel Press, New York, 1954.

Journals Consulted *

APRO Bulletin, Aerial Phenomena Research Organization, 3910 E. Kleindale Road, Tucson, Arizona 85712 U.S.A.

Canadian Aerial Phenomena Research Organization Bulletin, Winnipeg. **

Canadian UFO Report, P.O. Box 758, Duncan, British Columbia V9L 3Y1

CAPlC Reports, Canadian Aerial Phenomena Investigations Committee, Scarborough Ontario. **

Fate Magazine, 500 Hyacinth Place, Highland Park, Illinois 60035 U.S.A.

Flying Saucer Review, West Malling, Maidstone, Kent, England.

Flying Saucer Review. Case Histories. **

Inner Life, 214 Glengary Avenue, Toronto, Ontario M5M lE4

SUFO Bulletin, Saskatoon UFO Club. **

Saucers, Space & Science, Willowdale, Ontario. **

Topside, Ottawa, Ontario. **

UFO INFO, Bulletin du GESAG, Bruges, Belgium.

UFO-Quebec, 361 le Corbusier, Beloeil, Quebec J3G 3N8

** No longer published.

155